Praise for *The Ten-Minute Marriage Principle*

"THE TEN-MINUTE MARRIAGE PRINCIPLE provides invaluable tools every couple should know and apply. Whether you are newlywed or married sixty years, this must-read will deepen your relationship and foster a greater level of intimacy."
—Lisa Bevere, bestselling author, *Kissed the Girls and Made Them Cry*

"All marriages go through times of disaffection—times when you don't feel close. It is what you do during these times that makes or breaks the future of your relationship. THE TEN-MINUTE MARRIAGE PRINCIPLE is an awesome tool to keep your hearts close."
—Dr. Tim Clinton, president, American Association of Christian Counselors

"Douglas Weiss's excellent book, THE TEN-MINUTE MARRIAGE PRINCIPLE, offers profound insight into how we can better create bonds of matrimony that reflect God's marital design. It offers an array of practical and inspirational illustrations and exercises to expand your current views and beliefs regarding how marriage *really* works. It's an excellent, fun, and resourceful handbook that's full of creative, stimulating, and out-of-the-box strategies for refreshing and renewing your marital commitment!"
—Paula White, senior pastor of Without Walls International Church and author of *You're All That!*

The TEN-MINUTE MARRIAGE PRINCIPLE

Quick, Daily Steps for Refreshing Your Relationship

DOUGLAS WEISS, PhD

NEW YORK   BOSTON   NASHVILLE

Scriptures are taken from the HOLY BIBLE: NEW INTERNA-
TIONAL VERSION®. Copyright © 1973, 1978, 1984 by Interna-
tional Bible Society. Used by permission of Zondervan Publishing
House. All rights reserved.

Note: The testimonies of individuals in this book were created from
composites of clients who share similar issues. Names and identifying information have been changed to protect confidentiality. Any
similarity between the names and stories of individuals described in
this book and individuals known to readers is coincidental.

FaithWords
Hachette Book Group USA
237 Park Avenue
New York, NY 10017

Visit our Web site at www.faithwords.com.

Printed in the United States of America

First Edition: November 2007
10 9 8 7 6 5 4 3 2 1

FaithWords is a division of Hachette Book Group USA, Inc.

The FaithWords name and logo is a trademark of Hachette Book
Group USA, Inc.

Library of Congress Cataloging-in-Publication Data

Weiss, Douglas.
  The ten-minute marriage principle : quick, daily steps for
  refreshing your relationship / Douglas Weiss.—1st ed.
      p. cm.
  Summary: "A popular relationship expert offers these simple
yet revolutionary ways to build true intimacy in just minutes
each day"—Provided by publisher.
  ISBN-13: 978-0-446-69810-8
  ISBN-10: 0-446-69810-5
  1. Marriage—Religious aspects—Christianity. I. Title.
  BV835.W45 2007
  248.8'44—dc22
                                                    2007011201

To all of those who said "I do"
to the most amazing person they have ever met.

CONTENTS

The TEN-Minute
Marriage Principle

1
Ten Minutes—Really!

Sean and Kate were married for seventeen years. They had three children and life was good. Sean had a steady job and was liked at work. Kate made a part-time income with a home business and the children were doing well in their school.

As we all know, looks can be deceiving. During the past few years, the spark has begun to dwindle in their marriage. Kate feels that Sean works too much and doesn't really connect with her at home. Sean believes he has to work a lot to provide for their family's ever-growing bills and Kate doesn't understand his world of responsibility.

Sonya and Ben are a couple who also look good on the outside, but their secret is even deeper. Ben is busy with his company, employees, and hobbies. Sonya feels she has been raising their three girls by herself most of their twenty years of marriage. They have grown so far apart they call each other "friends." They're right, in that it has been two years since they have been physically intimate, although they still sleep in the same bed.

There are also couples like Ed and Sue, who not only look good on the outside but, in reality, are truly still in love. Sue is affectionate toward her husband in public and says positive things about him. Ed loves to be with Sue. He is helpful around the house, he takes her on dates, and he smiles just talking about his wife.

Ed and Sue, like Ben and Sonya, have been married for more than twenty years. They are also on the last phase of raising their teenage children. Ed works hard and Sue has worked part-time as a nurse on and off. They had life happen to them over their two decades together: health issues, tough financial times, and plenty of long talks about the children.

The difference for Ed and Sue is that they intuitively know how to have a loving marriage, or they somehow discovered the secrets to a successful marriage and are actually applying them. If you, like the first two couples, are struggling to enjoy marriage, you can discover a profound secret to a happy marriage and begin implementing it today.

A Change in Just Minutes a Day

Ten minutes a day, that's all I ask. I know it sounds odd, but really that one variable can make such a significant difference that it has astounded me for more than nineteen years in counseling couples.

Sean and Kate were able to apply the Ten-Minute Marriage Principle and the spark came back to their marriage. Even after two years of isolation, Sonya and

Ben applied the Ten-Minute Marriage Principle and in six weeks they were not only enjoying physical intimacy, but they really liked each other too!

The Ten-Minute Marriage Principle works! I have worked with couples far more desperate than Sonya and Ben or Kate and Sean. I have counseled couples who, for decades, had loveless and sexless marriages, and yes, within weeks of applying the Ten-Minute Marriage exercises they were enjoying their relationships again.

What is the principle? The Ten-Minute Marriage Principle is taking a few minutes each day with your spouse for some intimacy workouts. This is ten minutes of focused work that you and your spouse will do for your marriage to keep it fit and happier than it may have been for years.

I define the Ten-Minute Marriage Principle as "intimacy workouts" because these are comparable to physical workouts. Most of us have heard about the importance of working our core muscle groups. Those who have adopted routines to work those muscles have reported greater strength and endurance.

With the Ten-Minute Marriage Principle, the exercise routine I will introduce here will work on the core of your relationship. As the intimacy core muscles are strengthened daily, you can experience incredible closeness and endurance to run this marathon we call marriage.

To support your core strengthening, I have included support principles in this book so that not only your relational abs look great but your other muscles are toned up too.

Truth vs. Fiction

Why does the Ten-Minute Principle work? Because it is based upon the reality—not the fantasy—of marriage. When we are young, we often approach marriage idealistically. We say or think, *Our love will always be enough* or *I know he will always look at me that way* or a hundred other beliefs that time and circumstances challenge. We were young and naive. We didn't even know what we didn't know about marriage.

For example, I simply knew that when I was away from Lisa (then my future wife), my heart ached. I felt incomplete. When I was with her, I felt taller, more handsome, and fortified in an incredible way. That feeling was so strong, I wanted to have that connection my entire life. Lisa also had all kinds of such feelings and loved me more than she thought it was possible to love anyone. So we both knew what we knew—but we didn't know what we didn't know about marriage.

Lisa and I married during the marriage improvement movement, so we read many marriage books and thought we knew what we were in for. But reading a marriage book is very different from experiencing a real-life marriage.

Fantasy is common in Americans. Most of us fantasize about the bodies we'd like to have—even when we eat ice cream at 10:00 PM and our only form of exercise is pushing the buttons on the remote. As we keep gaining weight, we rationalize buying new clothes. We're living in a fantasy but want the reality of those who work out and watch their diets.

You see, if we watch too much television, we miss

many of the real story lines of success. You could define *success* as *consistent work in the same direction over decades*. People in reality-based marriages not only know that marriage is work, they do the work. Just as I know that if I want reasonable health, I have to work out.

HOW I KNOW IT WORKS

I live the Ten-Minute Marriage Principle. Lisa and I have been happily married for over twenty years now. Lisa comes from a godly home and is the last of six children. She is beautiful, godly, hardworking, and an incredible mother and a coworker in all that we do.

I, however, have a completely different story. I was conceived in adultery. That's not a great start for marital success. My mother's first husband divorced her, the man who helped create me abandoned her, and a third man married her before I was born, and his last name was Weiss. He was an alcoholic and, three children later, he and my mother divorced. I was placed in foster home after foster home for a while, then returned to my mother.

I became angry, addicted to various substances, and had all kinds of negative ideas about relationships. Then Christ came into my life and the healing process began. I went to Bible college and met Lisa. We dated for five years, during which we read every marriage book available. A year after I'd entered seminary, we married.

I tell you my story because I know some of you have hurts, addictions, or other issues that you think forfeit you from having a great marriage. It's not true. During my master's program in marriage and family counseling, I prayed for the ability to be intimate and to have a great marriage. I can't stand hypocrisy and I didn't want to ever give people suggestions that I wasn't doing or willing to do. God answered my prayer and gave me the great tool of the Ten-Minute Marriage Principle, which Lisa and I have practiced throughout our marriage.

I want every couple to be happy and successful in their relationship. As a counselor I know that, barring untreated addictions or mental illness, if a couple is willing to work, almost any marriage can be happy and healthy.

You can be a Ten-Minute Marriage Principle success story yourself. There are, however, three obstacles that can get in your way. I want to address these straight up in our first chapter.

THREE OBSTACLES TO SUCCESS WITH THE TEN-MINUTE MARRIAGE PRINCIPLE

1. PERSONALITY

I know we were all created differently and each person has his or her own personality. If you love your personality too much, though, you can't be successful in marriage. In giving us our personalities, God didn't want us to worship ourselves but to utilize our personalities to worship Him—and to express *His* personality through us.

People who like their own personalities too much constantly want their spouses to become more like them instead of more like Christ. The basic message is, "Until you become just like me, you're not measuring up."

If you wanted to marry someone just like you, it would have been much cheaper to marry yourself! You know—you'd have no conflicts, changes, or growth being enhanced by close contact with another personality.

People who like themselves too much have a mantra they use every time they are asked to do something they do not want to do: "That's not my personality." This can keep a person from benefiting from the Ten-Minute Marriage Principle. To be successful, you have to do things whether they are your "personality" or not. This is true in health, wealth, and relationships as well.

Early in my marriage to Lisa, I had a personal fitness trainer. You know, those big muscley guys at the gym whom you pay to work you out hard enough to reach your fitness goals.

One of my trainers was a Mr. Bodybuilder of some state. He was huge. If he told me to go on the leg press and do three sets of ten, you could imagine his face if I told him, "Matt, it's not my personality to do a leg press." He would laugh himself silly. "What does your personality have to do with pushing a weight? You push the weight, you get results, and if you don't push the weights, you won't get the results you are paying for."

Or say I go to a financial advisor. I tell him it's no longer "my personality" to save money for retirement. He, too, would laugh and say something like, "What does your personality have to do with it? You save now, you have wealth later. If not, you're broke at age sixty-five."

I know this sounds silly, but sometimes during a counseling session I recommend a certain exercise to a couple to get the change in relationship they're seeking and whammo, I get, "It's not my personality."

If you like your personality too much, you can limit your success in life. When I am speaking at marriage conferences I explain it like this: God made our personalities, but after the Fall, He, through the Holy Spirit, had one mission—to restore us to our original personalities, which are totally in His image. You see, God may like your personality, but He is committed to kill any part of you that doesn't look quite like Him.

So as I tell my clients and myself: don't hold on to *you* too tightly. What God has in mind is better than what our personalities try to limit us to.

Here's what I suggest as you go though this book: stay open-minded and openhearted and try the exercises I suggest. Forget whether they're consistent with your personality or not. Do them as directed and then you will be able to measure your results.

2. "FEELINGS FIRST" DECISION MAKING

Here is another culprit that can keep you from benefiting from the Ten-Minute Marriage Principle. I call it "Feelings First" Decision Making.

What I am talking about here is relying upon your feelings instead of your mind when you make decisions. If feelings rule what you decide to do, you won't be successful in marriage or in life long-term.

Here's what I mean. If you exercise only when you

feel like it, you will never benefit from exercise. If you pay your mortgage or credit card bills only when it's convenient, you will experience monetary difficulty that limits your future financial success.

I know it may sound silly, but some couples will do marriage enhancement exercises only when they "feel like it." Those couples will never enjoy sustained intimacy; rather they will go through ups and downs. When they are down, they will do marriage exercises. When they are up, they see no need to.

The fact is, many of us have moved from doing the right thing to doing what we feel like doing. Americans in general operate with their feelings first in decision making instead of by principle.

Every athlete hits a wall—the point where he doesn't feel like training anymore. The ones who obey their feelings and stop practicing find themselves thrown off the team. The ones who train because it's right, not because it feels good, over a sustained period of time are successful.

In the following pages, I will recommend various exercises. Again, if you do only what you feel like doing, you *cannot* maintain the benefits of the Ten-Minute Marriage Principle. If, however, regardless of how you feel, and even if you and your spouse don't like each other at the moment, you still decide to do the Ten-Minute Marriage Principle Exercises, you will experience a strengthening of your marriage that gives you the endurance to run a good race—all the way "till death do us part."

So don't succumb to your feelings. Do what you know is right, not what you feel is right.

3. WAITING FOR DESIRE

Kate and Ty were an attractive couple who were married for about ten years. They were professionals and had one small child. They came to me when a rift appeared in their relationship. We sat down together, trying to get to the root of their problem. After rejecting several of the ideas I offered, Kate blurted out, "I just don't desire to be married anymore."

I asked Kate if she was having an affair, and she assured me that this was not the case. Then I asked questions about her sleep, weight loss or gain, and energy level to see if maybe she was depressed. I also asked if anyone close to her had died or any other major life changes had occurred. She said, "No. I simply don't have a desire anymore for marriage."

As a counselor, I have heard this time and time again and usually from good people. Kate wasn't depressed, having an affair, or grieving, so what was making her want to leave her marriage? Kate, like so many Americans, has a paradigm problem when it comes to desire. This paradigm problem comes when you believe something that is not true.

I once had a seminary professor tell the class, "If you believe something is true, the results are real, whether it's actually true or not." For instance, if you believe someone at work or a neighbor doesn't like you, whether he does or not is irrelevant. You are going to behave as if he doesn't like you.

Kate believed that desire just happens: you either have desire or you don't. She thought that desire comes and goes and when it goes, well, it's gone. Obviously this paradigm problem can create a massive roadblock in a marriage!

Good news: I have found the secret to creating desire! You see, desire doesn't come first—desire comes second. *Desire is the direct result of a consistent discipline.* Take soda, coffee, or alcoholic beverages, for example. Many people drink one or all of these on a regular basis. They consistently have a desire for their beverages of choice because they have consistently consumed them—usually at the same time of day or in the same circumstances each time.

To create a desire, you simply have to create a discipline. Take, for example, carrot juice. If you drink carrot juice two to three times a day for a few weeks, you will actually begin to like and desire carrot juice without anyone's coaxing you into drinking it. The same is true of exercise. If you start running or going to the gym at 5:00 AM several times a week, in the beginning it will be tough, but once you surpass that the desire begins to grow. In a couple of months, your body wakes up for that five o'clock workout.

Desire is always second. What does all this talk about desire have to do with the Ten-Minute Marriage Principle? Everything!

If a husband and wife read the next chapter, choose three exercises for practicing the Ten-Minute Marriage Principle, and then don't discipline themselves, they will not build a strong desire to keep doing these exercises. They will flounder because the momentum of desire will not kick in for them.

This is like the person who buys a gym membership, goes three times, then misses a month. That person will never develop a desire to work out and will not be able to retain any level of fitness. Waiting for desire is an obstacle to success in the Ten-Minute Marriage Principle. If you can keep your commitment to ten minutes a day, then the desire for a great marriage will grow.

Those who push through from discipline to desire get the momentum they need to enjoy sustained marital happiness. It's as if the wind comes under your wings and it's not hard at all to do the Ten-Minute Marriage Principle Exercises you chose. Remember, Lisa and I have been doing these exercises for decades. There's no effort to it at all now. We just do them each day.

Kate agreed to do the Ten-Minute Marriage Principle. Even though she didn't enjoy marriage, she didn't want a divorce—so she was willing to work. She accepted the fact that changing her feelings would take daily work and time. Kate began working toward giving up ten minutes of her day, and so did Ty. They were faithful and sometimes Ty doubled up for what he called "extra results."

Now Kate has a new and consistent love for Ty, and he has a revived level of love for Kate as well. The friction and fussing have decreased so much they can now laugh about where they were even just a few months later. It's people like Kate and Ty who inspired me to write this book, so everyone can have the joy of laughing at the past as they are enjoying their present.

YOUR SUCCESS

The bottom line is, the Ten-Minute Marriage Principle Exercises work if you work them. You are holding a marriage manual that has already been tested in real marriages, even across cultures. I have traveled to several countries teaching these Ten-Minute Marriage Principle Exercises with the same positive results.

I have heard countless times, "We need a miracle. Without one, we will be divorced." Through applying these principles, many, many couples have been able to take control of their marital destinies and experience incredible relationships.

You must accept that marriage is not a fantasy—in reality, it's work. The work doesn't always have to be hard but it does have to be consistent. If you don't do consistent work, you tend to have to do the hard work. Let me give you an example.

I live in the mountains in Colorado Springs. I share my property with all kinds of weeds. Weeds are a manageable phenomenon if I am consistent. If I get out and spray or pull out the weeds when they are small, controlling them is not much effort at all. If, however, I become inconsistent, it becomes very hard work. I then have to get a shovel and sweat a lot. If I had taken the time weeks earlier, it would have taken a second or two.

Marriage is exactly the same way. If I am consistently doing the Ten-Minute Marriage Principle Exercises, I am working—but not hard. After all, it's only ten minutes! If, however, Lisa and I stop the exercises for a time, our intimacy will begin to erode. Then friction and not liking each other builds. The arguments and late-night "discussions" begin. You know what I mean!

You've heard the expression "You can pay now or you can pay later." That is so true with marriage. For Lisa and me, those ten minutes a day are a daily investment in our marriage. Making this investment month after month, year after year, decade after decade, insures that Lisa and I will be relationally wealthy. I know there will be days when Lisa or I may need to withdraw from our account. If we have contributed to our account daily, there will always be relational resources to cover the withdrawals when we need to make them.

THE TIME FRAME

Now let's talk about the ten minutes. Lisa and I are busy, just like everybody else. This year I will write a few books, speak at conferences nationally and internationally, appear in the media, run a full-time practice, meet with other therapists weekly in my office, go to church, help with homework, exercise, date Lisa, and have people over for birthdays along with all the other stuff of life we all get to do.

Yet with all this going on around us, Lisa and I will still take ten minutes where we are intentionally connecting. Lisa will never hear an excuse from me for not having ten minutes. I always have ten minutes to invest in my marriage. So do you.

I want to illustrate to you just how committed I am to the Ten-Minute Marriage Principle in my own life. Recently I was asked to do a marriage conference in

Norway. This conference was to be on live television and aired all over Scandinavia. When I arrived in Norway from my very, very long flight, I ate a short meal, had time to change, and was picked up to go to the studio. That night I spoke for two or more hours and went back to the hotel. It took me a while to figure out the international call system that I had to use in the hotel, but I did it. Why? So that I could do my daily marriage exercises with my wife. I was in Norway for a few days and my phone bill was over one hundred dollars!

The Ten-Minute Marriage Principle is a lifestyle decision. I always have time—it's how I use it. The way I use my time creates my positive desires or negative desires. I always want a desire to connect to Lisa. She is God's gift to me. My response to this gift should be so much more than ten minutes a day but rarely less than ten minutes a day.

You, too, deserve to enjoy the greatest marriage possible. I tell people I know that if they're going to eat, eat great food. The same is true about marriage. If you're going to be married, have a great marriage! Let me show you how.

2
THE TEN-MINUTE
EXERCISE MENU

So that you, too, can enjoy the results of the Ten-Minute Marriage Principle, I have put together a menu of exercises. Each exercise is designed to stimulate your marriage. Each exercise is unique, so you can pick and choose what makes sense for you to do at this time in your relationship.

In my work with couples for many years, I've found that most like the freedom to choose. Usually there is one internally motivated spouse (see chapter 6) who doesn't want to be told what to do—that person is better motivated by him- or herself than by others. I have also found that some couples have one or more relationship skills already developed. They can pick from a menu to strengthen another skill. And finally, there is the creativity factor. Some couples just like to try different things and be more spontaneous.

So, as you read through these pages, I want you to feel free to underline or put little smiley faces ☺ next to the exercises you are willing to try. In the next chapter you will be asked to commit to doing three exercises each day in order to practice the Ten-Minute Marriage Principle.

Remember, both of you have to exercise to build your marital core muscles. So be prepared to make a commitment to do some work. You can start your selection of exercises right away, which will make the rest of the book more fun for you. If you start today, by the time you finish the book you will already see positive changes occurring in your marriage!

THE MENU

EXERCISE #1: PRAYER

It may surprise you, but I've found that couples who are people of faith often do not pray together. Many go to church or spiritual services or events together, but at home, one-on-one, other than thanking God at meals, they don't pray together. Just yesterday a pastor and his wife were in my office. They have been active in ministry for more than twenty-five years. When I asked them about praying with each other, they sheepishly admitted that they very rarely do so.

I really believe in prayer. In my twenty-five-plus years of faith I have seen so many miracles that I have to conclude that prayer works. I think there is some truth to the saying, "A couple who prays together stays together."

The prayer I'm talking about is an out-loud conversation with God. When the disciples asked Jesus to teach them to pray, He said what we call the Lord's Prayer in Matthew 6:9–13.

I am not suggesting you recite the Lord's Prayer together. I am suggesting that you open your heart and mouth and just talk to God in the presence of your spouse. Some couples kneel, others walk around one another or hold hands. In whatever way you decide to do this, prayer is a great daily exercise. If you have not been connecting spiritually, I would definitely recommend this exercise to do daily as part of practicing the Ten-Minute Marriage Principle.

Prayer not only helps you to connect spiritually, but it can energize your marriage when God speaks back to both of you. It also helps you stay grateful to God for loaning His child to you in marriage. I personally like to thank God for Lisa in Lisa's presence. I think it keeps me in a more positive frame of mind for just how precious Lisa is, not just to me but to God as well.

EXERCISE #2: FLOODING

This is a very powerful exercise. You should try this once first before committing to doing it regularly. This exercise is only one minute long. You can set your kitchen or egg timer for a minute to let you know when the exercise is complete.

First, sit across from each other with knees close together. Second, maintain eye contact. Third, one person, say, "I love you" to the other person. Let's say Harry starts by saying, "I love you" to Sally. Then Sally has to let those words into her heart, not her head. This is critical. When she feels she has absorbed these words, she says, "Thank you." This way she verbally acknowledges this love deposit from Harry.

Then Sally says, "I love you" to Harry. After Harry lets the "I love you" sink into his heart, he says, "Thank you." Then he tells Sally again, "I love you," she says, "Thank you," then tells Harry, "I love you," then he says, "Thank you."

When doing this exercise, stick with just the words "I love you." Don't add to this or make it sexual in any way. The idea behind this exercise is that many of us know that our spouses love us. We say it all the time: "Love ya, babe," or "See ya, love ya." This is a great habit, but it's really good to soak in the love of your spouse.

There is a big difference between *knowing* someone loves you and *experiencing* that somebody loves you. As you do this exercise, you are really experiencing the love your husband or wife has for you. Your spouse is depositing his or her love intentionally in your heart, and you are intentionally letting that love into your heart.

I must warn you, some of you will laugh at first because you feel uncomfortable. Some of you will cry because your heart has so rarely experienced love this deeply. Either way, if you add this to your menu, it can be a very powerful one minute of your Ten-Minute Marriage Principle.

EXERCISE #3: GAZING

This exercise is amazing. As a counselor, I see so many couples who have difficulty even looking each other in the eyes. I have even had people not remember their spouses' eye colors!

Gazing is a very positive, strengthening Ten-Minute Marriage Principle exercise. As with the Flooding exercise, you will need a timer. You might start off at fifteen seconds, then go to thirty, forty-five, and to a minute. Some couples do this exercise for several minutes.

This exercise is quite simple. Get two chairs and sit across from each other. You can also do this on a sofa or in bed. Set your timer for how long you want to gaze. Then just sit and look into each other's eyes. That's right: just look. Absolutely no talking is involved.

This exercise can blow you away—some couples feel exponentially closer after doing this for a minute. You can experience the presence, personality, and power of your spouse in a tremendous manner.

The goal behind this exercise is to connect at a non-verbal, experiential level. You can connect to and experience your spouse without words. Doing this daily can really accelerate how connected you and your spouse feel to one another.

EXERCISE #4: FEELINGS

Before I move into the Feelings exercise I want to explain a few things. First, I designed this exercise for myself in my first year of marriage. So I know it's powerful. It can move someone from being an emotional illiterate to being a "black belt" expressing his feelings! Second, I believe so strongly that this skill is critical if you want to experience and maintain intimacy with your spouse. If you know you are one of those who has a hard time saying what you feel, whether you are male or female this would be a great pick for your Ten-Minute Menu.

Third, ever since I began writing—I started in 1993 and this is my twentieth book—I have included this exercise in almost every book. If you have seen it before, move ahead to the other exercises. If you haven't see this before, this is an important exercise to consider sometime during your marriage.

People who can't express their feelings become emotionally constipated. If either of you cannot identify or share feelings with the other, you will have so many more arguments and much more anger throughout your marriage. When spouses can't identify what they feel, the feelings build up and one of the two withdraws for hours or days or blows up. Both responses chip away at the relationship.

Where do we get trained to express feelings? Unless you learned it in your family growing up or in therapy, you may have a hard time with this at first. It would be great if every school or house of worship offered a class called Feelings 101. I mean, I have four degrees and nobody taught me how to identify or communicate feelings!

In Appendix A of this book, you will find a feelings list. For this exercise, choose a feeling from that list, then place that feeling in the following two sentences (or you can use the sample sentences I included with the exercise):

I recently felt _____ when ___[describe specific event]___ .

As a child or adolescent, I felt _____ when
[describe specific event] .

Let me give you an example. Say Harry chose the
word *excited*. His sentences might be something like
this:

I recently felt *excited* when *appearing on a national
television show*.
As an adolescent, I felt *excited* when *I rode a motorcycle for the first time at age fifteen*.

You see, what Harry is doing is using the same feeling word in a recent circumstance and in a past circumstance. He is practicing attaching the name of an
emotion to an experience in which he felt the emotion—
both now and earlier in his life.

Anyone using this exercise should do so for at least
three months to develop his or her emotional skill level.
After about three months, you can drop off the childhood memory example.

Because this exercise can create fireworks (and not
the good kind), be sure to stay within the following
boundaries when you are relating to each other.

Boundary #1. When doing this exercise, never, ever
use an example that involves your spouse or your marriage—even for the positive feelings words. If you don't
keep this boundary, this exercise will mutate into a way
for each of you to expose mostly negative feelings toward each other, and this will be counterproductive.
Two things will happen: you won't want to do the exer-

cise, and your relationship will stay at its current emotional level.

Keeping the examples of your feelings outside the marriage makes this exercise very safe. You know that you are not going to get zinged in any way by your spouse. Also, it is much easier to listen actively when you know you don't have to defend yourself about what might be said. So keep your spouse out of your example, and you can do this exercise for decades and still get positive results in your marriage.

Boundary #2. When doing the feelings exercises, maintain eye contact. Do not look up, down, or past your spouse but rather into your spouse. This boundary is critical if you want this exercise to be effective—to connect you heart to heart. So look at each other when you do this exercise.

Boundary #3. The third boundary of this exercise has to do with the time after one of you shares a feeling. You are to give no feedback to each other. You simply quietly listen, and when your spouse is finished sharing a feeling, you share yours. The point is just to get familiar with expressing your emotions to one another. Do two feelings a day as part of your practicing the Ten-Minute Marriage Principle.

Here is an example of a couple practicing the feelings exercise. Our couple's names are Holly and Max.

> MAX: I recently felt trusted when my boss pulled me aside and asked me what I really think about the current project that we were working on.

As an adolescent, I felt trusted when my brother told me how he felt about Diane, a girl he liked in high school.

HOLLY: I recently felt embarrassed when I didn't remember if I put my lipstick back on after I ate lunch.

As a child, I felt embarrassed when I was in second grade and I forgot some of my lines in a class presentation in front of all the parents.

MAX: I recently felt tough when I had to deal with a pushy salesperson trying to get me to buy something I didn't want.

As a child, I felt tough when a fifth-grader was picking on my friend and I pushed him on the ground and he left my friend alone.

HOLLY: I recently felt important when my boss was listening to every word I was saying and looking as if she understood.

As a child, I felt important when I was chosen for first chair in the clarinet section for band in sixth grade.

Here's an example of how powerful this exercise can be. A client who was using drugs and alcohol and visiting prostitutes came in for counseling. He and his wife practiced the Feelings exercise for six weeks, and they are feeling incredibly closer to each other. The husband actually started telling his guy friends about the Feelings exercises so that they also can do the exercises with their wives. You know that this exercise is powerful if guys are telling other guys to do it! This man gave up all of his addictions and is enjoying regular emotional intimacy with his wife. He recently told me, "If I had known my life could have been this good, I would have gotten help sooner!"

EXERCISE #5: MEMORY LANE

All of us like to stroll down memory lane. Whether you've been married months, years, or decades, you have incredible memories. Every couple experience the adventure of life together and keep memory "snapshots" of it in their minds.

I know you have had your fair share of less-than-wonderful encounters and memories as well. This exercise intentionally forces you both to focus on the positive moments. The purpose of this exercise is twofold: First, it will reinforce that you as a couple have had positive moments and when you remember these, it can create a more positive feeling in your marriage. Second, by reinforcing positive memories, you are much more apt to create more positive memories.

So, as part of your Ten-Minute Marriage Principle, each of you recalls one positive memory a day. Then face each other, look into each other's eyes, and share your positive memories about each other or the marriage.

Again, let me give you an example.

SHANE: I remember the time we went hiking together. We talked for hours and then we just held each other and fell asleep for about an hour. I felt so close to you. I was glad you were my wife.

ALICIA: I remember the day after I finished a semester of college. You drove forty minutes one way to get me some Krispy Kreme doughnuts and brought them to me early that morning.

This is a very fun exercise. Lisa and I just did this exercise together again, and this one always puts a smile on our faces. Life is busy and sometimes chaotic. These exercises can be the calm and warmth in a day of your life. This exercise takes very little time, so it easily will fit into your Ten-Minute Marriage Principle.

EXERCISE #6: THE TWO E'S

This is a fun exercise to help spouses interact more meaningfully at the end of the day. Often spouses are separated for many hours by work and other responsibilities. During these hours, your spouse will experience a myriad of thoughts, feelings, circumstances, and interactions. You know how it can be after you both finally get back together after a long day apart: The wife asks her husband, "So how was your day?" and gets a monotone "Fine." The husband asks his wife, "So how was your day?" and gets a similar response. Then the two of you go on without ever talking in depth.

As a counselor, I have known couples who interact like that day after day, year after year. When that happens, feelings of aloneness, separation, and even indifference can creep into a marriage.

The Two E's can help this conversation with your spouse go into a slightly different direction. With the Two E's you share two specific occurrences in your day so your spouse gets some window into where you have been and what you've been doing. The E's stand for *Energized* and *Effort*. Share with your spouse something that energized you and something that called for effort.

When you do the Two E's, face each other and keep eye contact. Keep your sharing to something that did not involve your spouse.

Let's look at an example.

ELI: Today I was energized by one of my coworkers. He was sharing how he used the ideas I had shared with him over lunch last week meeting with sales. He closed a good account and he actually told the owner that I had a part in that.

Today work was an effort for me because I was stuck in traffic due to construction, and that caused me to get behind. I really didn't catch up for a couple of hours. Just sitting stuck in the car—it took every ounce of strength not to scream!

VANESSA: I was energized today when I talked to my sister Carol. She was so excited about Jon. Jon started to walk yesterday. It reminded me of when our children started to walk and just how fast the years go by.

It took effort for me not to break the phone when I was dealing with the mortgage company. They had voice-mail menus, and three times in a row I was disconnected.

You can see that this is just sharing a slice of your day with your spouse. This exercise takes a very small

amount of time to do, but it can really make a difference. Both of you can feel like a part of each other's day.
I warn you, though: you can really get into this exercise
and talk about the other parts of your day as well! As a
counselor, I say the more sharing, the better!

EXERCISE #7 MY LOVE LETTER

This is a fun exercise. If you are spontaneous and creative, you might like to do this one often. If you find
it difficult to put your love and appreciation in words,
this exercise offers you a great opportunity to work out
those creative muscles.

I'm sure you have a whole lot of love for your spouse.
But time can wear on your love, and without positive
reinforcement you can both end up feeling drained and
dry about each other.

You may be thinking that writing a love letter every
day could take some time. That's true, but the Love Letter exercise is actually spoken, not written. So it won't
take as long as you think.

Now I know some of you, whether male or female,
are thinking I am asking for pages of poetic rhythm and
rhymes. I assure you that is not the point at all in this
exercise. The point is to creatively, verbally share a loving thought you have about your spouse.

Most of us think about how we love our spouses
throughout the week. This exercise just helps you put
that love in words your spouse hears and absorbs. And
when your spouse does this exercise, you get to hear
how much you are loved as well.

What I love about this exercise is that it forces me

to think about my love for Lisa regularly. This exercise intentionally reinforces both spouses in how much they love each other.

For this exercise, face each other and maintain eye contact. One spouse complete this sentence: "If I were writing a love letter today to you, it would say. . . ." After he or she has completed his or her love letter, the other spouse completes the same sentence.

Here's an example.

JAMES: If I were writing a love letter today to you, it would say that I loved you before I met you. When I met you, the beauty of your heart captivated me. I love just watching who you are—mother, friend, and lover—so to say "I love you" is too small, for I am still discovering the beauty you are.

It's okay, men, if your love letter is different. After all, you are you, and you are the one she loves. Here's another example.

JACKIE: If I were writing a love letter today to you, it would have to say "Thank you." I don't know that I have ever said "Thank you" for holding me when my world or heart is coming apart. Thank you for all the mundane, everyday things you always do, and thank you that you do all of these things without the many thank-yous that you deserve to hear!

This exercise is another one that can blow you away. No matter what happened that day, you could be fortified by having your spouse speak his or her love letter to you. I offer you this friendly warning: during this exercise the warmth and "wow" feelings you may experience can lead to hugs, kisses, and other reactions!

The fact is that we all are so in love, but we don't regularly prime the pump—say how we feel. This exercise communicates the depth of our feelings and appreciation to our spouses. When you do this regularly, all of life seems just a little easier, burdens lighter, and life just so much sweeter.

EXERCISE #8: GRATEFUL STATEMENTS

To have a positive marriage, you have to plant positive seeds. I am always amazed, especially at couples in the community of faith, who understand the concept of reaping and sowing yet never apply it in marriage. The fact is, if you sow only negative seeds, you will eventually get a negative harvest.

Gratefulness is one of those positive seeds we can plant again and again. Grateful people find that good and positive things tend to happen in their lives. I want you to have good and positive things happen in your marriage.

Face each other and give each other eye contact. Take turns completing this sentence: "Today I am grateful for . . ." Do this twice.

When talking about gratitude, you can include your spouse some of the time, but keep your whole life in mind. Open up your heart to the many things you are and can be grateful for. Let's look at some examples.

WATSON: I am grateful today for how the Lord provided me favor with a client that can mean more business and money for us.

YOLANDA: I am grateful that I got off work early enough to watch the kids' game.

WATSON: I was grateful for our children's health and strength today. Even the coach commented on how well they did.

YOLANDA: I am grateful that we are a team. I feel we intuitively know when the other needs help.

Gratitude is contagious. If you consistently practice gratefulness with your spouse, you will begin to see so much more that you are thankful for. When you make gratefulness part of your Ten-Minute Marriage Principle Exercises, that vitamin can stimulate you both into a more positive and appreciative lifestyle. You can see why I added this as part of your menu!

EXERCISE #9: PLAY *WINNING@MARRIAGE*

You may be aware of my television show on TBN called *Winning@Marriage*. This is sort of a Christian *Newlywed Game* show, though we have couples who have been married from just months to more than sixty years. We send half the spouses backstage, and the ones remaining answer questions. Then the spouses who have been sequestered have to guess how their spouses answered.

This is one of the most interesting media adventures I've had, and I have had a lot! We tape three to four thirty-minute shows in a day. By the end of the day, my stomach hurts from laughing so hard. And even though we give points and a prize, couples have as much fun as I do. Also, I've found couples are actually learning about each other as they play the game.

To do this exercise, you can start with the questions that appear in Appendix B. For more questions, visit our Web site *www.tenminutemarriage.com* and download the same questions we use on the show. Pick a question and write down your answer. Have your spouse guess your answer.

In this exercise, you will definitely learn and laugh at the same time. My experience is that until a question is asked, you really don't know what your spouse's answer might be, so playing the game can be a fun part of your Ten-Minute Marriage Principle.

EXERCISE #10: WHAT I LEARNED

I am sure you have heard someone say, "I learn something new every day." I know this is absolutely true if you are living with an open heart. Life is constantly throwing us challenges, experiences, relationships, and changes in relationships that give us great opportunities to learn.

If you and your spouse are learning daily, you can capitalize on this daily. Since you are already learning, all you have to do is get skilled at sharing it. This is a great way to keep up with your spouse as he or she transforms over time.

In this exercise, face each other while doing the exercise and maintain eye contact. Have one person complete one of the following statements, then the other spouse complete another statement. Repeat this process once.

- Something I learned from God today was. . . .
- Something I learned from you today was. . . .
- Something I learned from others today was. . . .
- Something I learned about myself today was. . . .

If you use your spouse as an example, you *must say something positive*. Dan and Elly will be our example couple.

DAN: Something I learned from God today was that He listens to even my small prayers. I prayed about getting a break, and the boss told me to go home early because he was seeing too much of me and laughed.

ELLY: Something I learned about myself was that sometimes it's hard to be honest. A girl rang up the wrong sandwich today at lunch and it was more than a dollar less than the one I ordered. When I pointed it out, she said, "Never mind, I'll still give you the right sandwich." I was tempted to leave it at that, but I asked her to make it right on the check anyway.

DAN: Something I learned from you was to be positive toward people. You do this so naturally. I tried it for three days at work on George, who's always so negative. He actually smiled today and I thought that was great!

ELLY: Something I learned from someone else today is that being quiet is sometimes better than speaking your mind. I was in a meeting at work and Stephanie shot off what she thought about the owner's ideas. Well, he didn't really like her bluntness. He corrected her in front of everybody and said to think before we give any feedback to ideas that take more than a minute to create.

It's obvious how learning what your spouse is learning can help you stay connected.

That's the end of the menu. There are many relationship-building delicacies for you to choose from. Each exercise can take from a minute up to three or four minutes, and you can easily do several daily in ten minutes. I must warn you, however, that some couples keep talking after the ten minutes are up! If this happens with you, you are on your way to a great, lasting, loving marriage.

In the next chapter I will explain how to utilize your menu and maximize your exercises to have an incredible relationship.

3

MAKING THE
TEN MINUTES WORK

When I visit my favorite restaurants, I like reading the menus. I love deciding on the dessert or appetizer, then moving to a main course. I like choosing between duck, lamb, steak, or seafood. That's exactly where you are in this book. In the previous chapter I gave you ten menu options. In this chapter you get to pick your meal items from your Ten-Minute Menu.

Just this week I met with my psychologist friend. We meet regularly and usually go to the same restaurant. This time I suggested we try a new restaurant. Gary agreed, so we went there, sat down, and received a great menu. We both read through all the items offered, oohing and aahing at the exotic fare.

There were several very appetizing items on the menu. We ate our different dishes, each admiring the other's plate. Halfway through our lunch I suggested to Gary, "Hey, why don't we meet here for a while? I would like to try several items on the menu." He agreed.

When you look at the Ten-Minute Marriage Principle Menu, you might feel the same way as I did at the restaurant. You want to do them all! Well, you have a whole lifetime to try the different exercises. You might pick a few and find that they work for years, or you might want to work your way through the menu. Either way is good. When the food is good, any way you eat it is good!

First I will help you make your selections. Then I will also give you some tips to help you become successful in turning your ten minutes a day into an incredibly different marriage.

Your Selection

Let's go over your menu options so you can begin. I will list them for you here so you can check off the choices you would like to try for the next thirty to sixty days. This way you can start with something you both like.

He Likes   **She Likes**

_____   Prayer   _____

_____   Flooding   _____

_____   Gazing   _____

_____   Feelings   _____

_____   Memory Lane   _____

_____   The Two E's   _____

_____   My Love Letter   _____

_____   Grateful Statements   _____
_____   Playing *Winning@Marriage*   _____
_____   What I Learned   _____

I know it may be difficult, but you need to pick just three exercises to start with. While I know most restaurants don't encourage you to try a little of each meal before you order, it's a good idea to stop reading and actually try the exercises on the menu before you make your ultimate selections. This can make it more fun. This can also help you see the positive impact a few minutes' investment in your marriage can make. Once you know you can feel that close, you will be sold on the Ten-Minute Marriage Principle!

Today I went to Maggie Moo's ice cream store. They had a new flavor I hadn't tried before: chocolate peanut butter. So I asked for a taste. The employee grabbed one of those tiny tasting spoons and scooped a sample of the ice cream. As soon as the ice cream hit my mouth, I knew I would order it.

If I hadn't taken the time and the risk, I might have ordered a flavor I'd had before. This is not a bad thing, but discovering something new is always exciting! It adds variety to life. So I encourage you to try at least most of the exercises before you continue.

Here is another checklist of the exercises. Once you have tried them, just write a date by the exercise. In this way you will know that you have tried it and can compare to see which ones you both liked best.

Exercise	Date
Prayer	_____
Flooding	_____
Gazing	_____
Feelings	_____
Memory Lane	_____
Two E's	_____
Love Letters	_____
Grateful Statements	_____
Playing *Winning@Marriage*	_____
What I Learned	_____

THE MOMENT OF DECISION

Hopefully you tried all of the exercises that appealed to you. Now comes the moment of decision. Once the waiter or waitress has served your drinks, he or she asks you, "So what will it be tonight?" It is time to decide. As a couple, agree on three exercises you would like to try.

The three daily exercises we will start with are:

1. _____

2. _____

3. _____

Congratulations! You have taken the first important step in the Ten-Minute Marriage Principle. Now you get to connect your exercises to a point in time. So the next step for you to become successful using the Ten-Minute Marriage Principle is for you to decide *when* you can actually do these exercises.

As a counselor, I've seen that often one person in a marriage is a morning person and the other is usually a night owl. I also know sometimes a spouse is neither a morning nor an evening person. Let's try to be specific. You both know your schedules and your moods. What is a good time for both of you to commit to the ten minutes it will take you to do the exercises you just chose?

Remember that these are your relational core exercises. Ten minutes each day is what you are committing to so that your marriage can stay strong and fit for the marathon you have ahead of you. Making the decision as to when you will do this together is critical—if you commit to doing the exercises and make the time to do them, in years to come you will still look into each other's eyes, say, "I love you," and mean it from your heart. So below, write the time your workout should take place. Of course, you can always be early but try not to be late too often.

We will do our Ten-Minute Marriage Principle Exercises at:

_____ AM.

_____ PM.

Great! Now that you have decided what exercises and what time you will do them, you need to agree on a start date for this process. I find it very helpful for couples to write down a start date, first, because it helps them both to commit to start on that day, and second, they can always come back to this page to remind themselves when they started so that they know if they went their full thirty or sixty days. Couples can then see if they want to exchange an exercise for the next month or two.

Below, write the date you are committing to start your exercises.

We are starting our Ten-Minute Marriage Principle exercises on:

_____

TIPS FOR SUCCESS

I have learned that in most areas, there are ways to improve your success ratio, regardless of whether you are trying to pursue better health, wealth, relationships, or education.

When I was working on a master's degree, I learned some great tips. I learned to compare classes before choosing one. I found out that before I selected classes, I could get the syllabus each professor had for, say, Counseling 101. I could compare syllabuses and find out which professor was more realistic in his or her assignments. I also learned I could begin those assignments before the first day of class. These tips made completing the rest of my education smoother and much more successful.

In the same way, I want to give you a few tips that can heighten your success as you take your exercises from theory to practice. You deserve to be successful, so I hope these tips will help you reach your goal of a great marriage.

TIP #1: KEEP TRACK OF YOUR PROGRESS

I have taught couples in different countries and all over the United States how to win at marriage. Those who grabbed the bull by the horns and followed through by doing the exercises found the successful results they were looking for. But I have had too many conversations with couples in counseling or at conferences who are now back in the same cold, distant marriages they were in prior to the conferences or counseling.

When I ask what happened, they sheepishly admit, "We stopped doing the exercises." One way to stay with what you've committed to do is to keep track of your daily Ten-Minute Exercises. This will make you accountable for the decision you have made together. In Appendix C you will find a chart to use to keep track of your success.

If you'd rather, take a sheet of tablet paper and make your own daily Ten-Minute Exercises sheet. I personally like to tape my sheets on my mirror where I shave. This helps me to remember and keeps me honest. Or you can keep this book open to the appendix page to help your memory. Whatever works for you is a great tool for your success. Take a minute to choose how you will keep track of your Ten-Minute Exercises. Complete this sentence here or on your own sheet of paper.

Our approach to keep track of our Ten-Minute Marriage Principle Exercises is to _____

_____.

TIP #2: COMPETE WITH OTHER COUPLES

Here is a fun way to improve more than one marriage at a time! I often recommend this tip to keep couples making progress months and years down the road. Most people like friendly (I repeat, *friendly*) competition. In this competition everybody who participates is a winner, but there are also some prizes along the way.

Get another couple or several couples together and compete on who does their three-minute dailies the most consistently. Each couple keeps an honest record of how they are doing. You can e-mail them to each other or just call each other. The couple with the least number of days of doing their exercises can buy everyone dinner or have everyone over to their house for dinner.

I have seen churches with small groups apply the competition principle, and it really ends up being successful. I think just being accountable to other people keeps you additionally motivated. I personally use competition or accountability to push me to reach a goal or improve something in my life. For me, whether it's exercising or writing books, competition and accountability help a lot to get me where I want to go.

A more successful marriage is only ten minutes a

day away. You have the ten minutes a day to give to one of your most important relationships, so compete and maybe even get a free meal or two as you go!

TIP #3: SET UP CONSEQUENCES FOR SKIPPING EXERCISES

Some couples don't have couple friends close by geographically to engage in a competition. If you are not competing, this principle can be helpful for you. What you do is set your goal for daily doing the Ten-Minute Exercises. Then, set up a way to keep record of your progress. If you fall short of your goal, set up a consequence. Here are some examples of consequences that other couples have come up with:

- Two hours of home projects
- Two hours of cleaning out the garage
- A three-mile walk
- Giving money to a group you don't support
- Burning money (small amounts)
- No television for a week or two

The first or second time you find yourself having to deal with a consequence, you will see the power of this principle. Consequences help you stay motivated to keep your word on the Ten-Minute Exercises.

TIP #4: SET UP REWARDS FOR DOING EXERCISES

Some couples do better with rewards than with consequences. Here you set a reasonable goal for how consistent you need to be over a period of time, like sixty or ninety days. If you are consistent for your planned length of time, you will already be experiencing very positive rewards in your day-to-day life with your spouse. You will like being around him or her, and you will feel as if he or she likes you more as well.

You can set up rewards for being successful in following through on doing your Ten-Minute Exercises. Some examples of rewards couples have chosen for themselves are:

- A night at a bed and breakfast
- Dinner at a romantic restaurant
- A night at home with no children
- Each gets money to spend and shop
- A new piece of furniture
- A small adventure

As I mentioned in the Consequences principle, you probably want to keep track of your progress in some measurable way. Seeing your progress on a daily basis can be a visual aid and keep your motivation high. Some people attach a picture of whatever their reward is to their tracking sheet to even make it more fun.

TIP #5: OPERATE BY PRINCIPLE, NOT FEELING

I've mentioned that you will be tempted not to donate the ten minutes a day to make your marriage vibrant. Again, principle *or* emotion will be your guiding light. If you choose to operate by principle, you will do your Ten-Minute Exercises unless there is an absolute emergency.

An emergency *isn't* being tired, having a headache, or not liking your spouse for whatever reason that day.

Just this last week I had a couple come in for some intense counseling. The husband completed a polygraph exam in my office to verify the length and depth of his infidelity. The test results revealed some information the wife was not aware of. They had a difficult day. That night, the man initiated his three daily exercises. This not only turned that night around, but it also showed them that investing in a marriage even on a bad day can pay off big-time.

I've already mentioned that you and I have to choose principle over emotions not only in our marriage exercises, but in so many other areas of our lives. We have to decide via principle or emotions with food, physical exercise, money, and how we speak to people. I know that sometimes principles are tough to stick to when emotions start churning. I am so glad Lisa and I do our three Ten-Minute Exercises regardless of how we feel. In our many years together, there have been quite a few days when difficulties came our way—difficulties with life, relationships, or even each other. Regardless, we would do our exercises, and this usually helped to get us through those seasons. Like us, you will be tempted, but don't succumb to your emotions. Do your daily Ten-Minute Exercises.

Again, without consistency these exercises will not give you the momentum to take your marriage to a higher level. Let me give you an analogy. Suppose you broke your arm. You go to the hospital and you get a cast put on. A cast is just a structure. If the structure (cast) stays consistent day after day, healing occurs, and then it's possible to live life as if the arm was never broken at all.

Just a couple of years ago, I fell off my bike and broke my pinky finger. After X-rays, I was sent to a specialist. My pinky finger bulged, and the doctor said it would stay that way my whole life unless I could do one thing. He continued talking as I was looking at my hideous pinky. He said I would have to wear a brace day and night, without taking it off for six weeks. The brace wasn't that pretty either. I explained that I was hosting my own television show and he was clear: "You take it off, you might as well have never worn it a day."

Then he said, "In all my years, I've never had anyone do this successfully. So if you don't want to, it's okay." Something deep down inside of me was determined to show him that I could do such a simple thing. Well, it sounded simpler than it was. Every day as I took tape off to put new tape on, I had to decide: *Do I wear this ugly brace or not?* Well, I made my decision, based on principle, for six weeks.

Lisa and I went back to the doctor. He congratulated me for being successful. He then removed the brace. He wiggled the pinky around; not only could it move as it should, it was beautiful again with no hideous bulge.

Needless to say, I want you to have the most beautiful marriage possible. Consistency with the Ten-Minute Exercises has the potential to give both of you a much more fulfilling and rewarding marriage.

A great anything, including marriage, is daily work. If you do your daily marriage work, you will experience each other in a new way that will make those ten minutes seem like nothing for all the happiness you will gain. So follow these principles to insure your success in applying the Ten-Minute Marriage Principle. I know that you can do this; it's only ten minutes!

Let's review your plan for success.

- Decide which exercises to do.
- Decide when you are doing your exercises.
- Keep track of your progress.
- Compete with other couples.
- Set up consequences for skipping exercises.
- Set up rewards for doing exercises.
- Operate by principle, not feelings.

You have the exercises; you have a plan that can work. You have a way of keeping track of your progress and some ideas to keep you motivated to reach your goals. You are all set to start living the Ten-Minute Marriage Principle.

I encourage you to start right away. In the chapters to come are many ideas to help you to have a smoother marriage. Combine your exercises with the ideas ahead of you, and you're in for an exciting ride. So read, talk, and take steps when you need to, and above all, stay steady with your exercises!

The Ten-Minute Exercises are critical for a happy and satisfying marriage, but you will also benefit by exercising the other muscles of your relational body. I want you not only to have great abs and strong lower back, figuratively speaking, but it's even better if your legs, arms, chest, shoulders, and upper back are strong as well.

This analogy reminds me of a man who worked out

at a gym that I went to when I lived in Texas. He was at the gym almost every morning. He was consistent. I never saw him do aerobics or stretches. Peculiarly, he almost exclusively worked his arms. Granted, he probably had nineteen-inch arms, but his legs were scrawny and his chest and back were very average. He looked odd, really.

Now that we have your core muscles getting stronger, work the support structures to maximize your marriage. As you get better at relating to each other, you will look and feel better—just as physical exercise makes you look and feel better.

Let's now look at ways that, along with the Ten-Minute Marriage Principle, you can fortify your relationship.

4

WHAT GOVERNMENT ART THOU?

In following the Ten-Minute Marriage Principle, you will experience an amazing increase in closeness. I have seen so many marriages transformed just by the couples' applying themselves ten minutes a day. I guess it's true that whatever you do for ten minutes a day, you can become really good at.

But even a husband and wife who are enjoying better intimacy can still have some systems in their marriage that are not functioning at all, or are not optimal. If a system isn't working well, the couple will experience repeated conflict.

Let me give you an example. Charlie was an English professor at a local university. He was a sought-out editor and was brilliant with words. But Charlie had a bad habit (system) when it came to his car keys.

When Charlie went home, he would place his car keys almost anywhere but rarely in the same place twice. Consequently, each morning Charlie would spend fifteen to twenty minutes trying to find his keys. He would get mad at himself, the situation, and even his wife when he couldn't find the keys.

Charlie maintained this bad habit day after day, year after year. His wife actually stopped helping him look for the keys after their third year of marriage. He and his family were frequently late to social gatherings and appointments, which caused lots of embarrassment.

Charlie's dysfunctional system created much more stress in his life, marriage, and family. Charlie wasn't a bad person, but he had a bad system. Once Charlie agreed to put his keys on a key holder right by the garage door, every day he added peace to his life—and to his family's lives.

Systems are very important to evaluate and adapt in a marriage. Many of these systems of ways for doing things can impact marriages for years to come. So, to enhance your use of the Ten-Minute Marriage Principle, I am going to have you evaluate some major systems and maybe adopt some successful strategies to have an even better marriage. The first of these systems I call "government." Take a look.

WHO MAKES THE DECISIONS?

CHAD AND CINDY

Chad and Cindy were your everyday nice couple. Both were in their early thirties and they had two beautiful boys. The entire family was active in church. Cindy was in the choir and helped with some of the women's ministry work. Chad was in charge of the men's breakfasts and also helped with the kids' program that both their boys attended regularly.

Chad had a corporate management job and made a steady income, while Cindy was a substitute teacher who taught occasionally for additional income and to keep her teaching certificate active. They both loved God, each other, and their boys. Everything seemed to be going well for them. Neither Chad nor Cindy had any deep, dark secrets from the past. They were both raised in relatively healthy Christian homes.

So why were they in my office or, better yet, why am I writing about them in this book? They had a problem they could never seem to work through on their own. Chad and Cindy are not alone in this situation; many other couples have this same problem.

The problem was, even though Chad had a stable job and they lived within their means, Chad fancied himself as somewhat of an entrepreneur.

There's no wonder he had this tendency, because Chad's dad made a very good living by starting companies and buying real estate. Chad envisioned himself taking vacations whenever he wanted instead of the basic two weeks that he earned through the office.

So, periodically Chad would come up with another get-rich-quick scheme. He discussed starting various multilevel sales companies and a refurbishing company, investing in real estate, and buying Internet companies. After meeting with a potential business partner, Chad always had another "idea of a lifetime." He was charged up about finally being financially free, rich, and able to leap tall buildings in a single bound.

Some of you know exactly what I am talking about.

Lisa and I call them "change the world ideas." Many men have this affliction from time to time.

Chad assumed that Cindy would just go along with his scheme; after all, anyone with any business sense could see this was going to be a big opportunity. He explained to her all the money-building options they could try with their savings.

But Cindy responded by drilling him on how all the money they had saved suddenly became his to risk. And when did he come to the conclusion that he was the one to make all of their large financial decisions?

Chad cunningly switched gears and went through a list of concessions to convince her to say yes to his new business proposition. Feeling desperate, he resorted to saying, "I believe this is God's will." Cindy was not so sure, because she didn't have peace about the idea. Reluctantly, they went to bed feeling distant, angry, and frustrated with one another.

FRANK AND ANNA

Frank and Anna also are having some difficulty. They are in their late fifties. Their children are grown and married, and Frank and Anna have two grandchildren. Frank and Anna are both attractive and still physically active. They take daily walks and own a local company that has done well. Their retirement is in place and they enjoy traveling several times during the year.

They go to a Bible-believing church and are friends with the pastors. Over the years they have volunteered in almost every department of this church. Two years ago they were unanimously voted in as elders.

So what's the problem? Unlike Chad and Cindy, Frank and Anna don't have cycles of the same discussions over and over again. Instead they bicker. Daily they fuss, challenge, negotiate, or have short debates on petty issues. The topics of this bickering are embarrassingly small: how things are being done around the house and who should do them; what gets planted in their garden; when spring-cleaning should occur and who will do it; what restaurant they will go to; and when they will visit the children.

They love each other, God, their church, their family, and especially their two grandchildren. But Frank and Anna have a problem. Their problem is exactly the same silent killer of joy and peace that Chad and Cindy have.

This problem is also the creator of thousands of hours of unnecessary conflict. Both couples, Chad and Cindy and Frank and Anna, have not answered the basic question: *what government art thou?*

I travel regularly to speak at conferences. There's a point in each conference that I ask this very basic but profound question. The audience response is always the same. It doesn't matter if I'm in Connecticut, Texas, Florida, or California; they all give me a blank look. If you're wearing such a look now, keep reading.

A GOVERNMENT

A government, in its simplest form, is a structure that provides the ability and pathway to make decisions. A couple with a clear system of government have a clearer path to decisions, face less conflict, and create more time to be productive.

Like Charlie, who kept losing his keys, many couples have created a chaotic system through which they make decisions in their marriage. Sometimes it's the person who has more energy, who's louder, who's meaner, or who can remember more mistakes who wins. Most of us can relate to this chaotic decision-making process (a bad system).

When Charlie identified a new system (hanging up the keys daily), he created an order in his life that helped the entire family. Deciding "what government thou art" can also have a huge impact in your marriage as you are enjoying the Ten-Minute Marriage Principle in your life.

Chad and Cindy had no structure (government) in place to help guide them through a large decision. What happens when a couple has established no clear government? They choose a default system of chaos and manipulation. In this system, the winner is whoever can fight harder and longer, withhold more or withhold longer, or bring more people to their side of the war.

The chaos/manipulation system creates great casualties. Even if you "win," the other person has to lose for you to get your way. But nobody really wins. Chaos and manipulation can go on for years without anything getting settled.

Not only does a couple fail to settle issues, they can actually create wounds that can take years to heal. Chaos as a governing principle is not the best choice for anyone who wants his or her marriage to be successful.

It reminds me of a game we used to play as children; I'm sure some of you (especially the men) have played this. The game is called King of the Mountain. To play you need a huge mound of fresh earth. Then you need a few people who all want to be king of the mountain. Once the person gets to the top, everyone else's goal is to pull him or her off the mountain by any means possible.

You can create alliances and then grab a leg and drag this king down the hill. You can run full speed and crash into him and use momentum to dethrone him or her. Regardless, nobody stays king forever and everybody is able to get really, really dirty. A game every mother loves!

Yet many Christian marriages have this chaotic manipulation system in place. Why, you ask? Basically they have never sat down and decided how they will make decisions. What I mean is they never decided on a government that is greater than either of them individually.

For most couples it's simply a lack of knowledge. Others really like fighting, manipulating, and dethroning each other. It provides the whole family with entertainment. Picture it now: Mom and Dad are center stage and the audience, the four children, is soaking up this education on marriage. The exact agenda is irrelevant. Let's just watch them go at it.

First Dad's the king—no, no it's Mom, she tells Dad he's just like his dad and shoots off a few examples. Whammo! Mom didn't see her past coming up and Dad throws her down. Mom gets a running start and whack, they are both down. They go back to their corners (the bedroom and garage), and that's the show for tonight.

The problem with this little show is it teaches their kids how not to have a government *and* how to be unhappily married. Take the time to establish a marriage government. This government will be a very important support to your practicing the Ten-Minute Marriage Principle. How? Once you as a couple decide how you will make decisions and stick to your plan, you will be amazed at how much time and energy you will have to do more things than argue—such as your Ten-Minute Exercises.

When Charlie changed from an inefficient system to an efficient system, he and his family arrived at places on time (a big stress reliever). He spent less time searching for keys and more time improving his relationships. Once Chad and Cindy chose a government, they no longer had drawn-out fights over big stuff that ended up zapping their entire family for days. Frank and Anna bicker so little now they added weekend getaways to their travel portfolio.

A couple without a government is one that can be constantly in and out of the pastor's or counselor's office. A couple without a structure in place on how they will make decisions will face many hours of unnecessary gridlock.

I know some couples love chaos because they can vent and make up like teenagers. For most of us, however, life is too short to fuss more than we have to with the ones we love the most. So let's continue our discussion on governments.

A STORY OF GOVERNMENT

Before we go further, I want to make clear that every government will work as far as making decisions. The God of heaven and earth has used every form of government in time to carry out different aspects of His will on Planet Earth.

In order to discuss the various governments that are available for couples to choose from, we must take a walk. It's not a walk in the park but more like a walk down memory lane. This is no ordinary memory lane. This one starts before time and continues to the present moment.

In my book *Intimacy: A 100-Day Guide to Lasting Relationships*, I briefly discuss the idea of government as it relates to money. But government relates powerfully to how a couple interacts together as well. So, I want to show you, with an open heart and mind, the various forms of governments utilized in time.

PRETIME GOVERNMENT

Before time was made, God existed. Before one atom of the earth was created, God existed. As Christians, we believe in God the Father, God the Son (Christ), and God the Holy Spirit. Somehow the various expressions of God's government have always been there and always will be. Neither I nor anybody else really knows exactly how this government works; we have never seen its exact replication on earth.

The three-in-one Godhead appears, however, to operate on some basic idea of equality and respect. So I offer this government as God's government existing prior to the creation of time, Earth, and Adam and Eve.

THE FIRST-IN-TIME GOVERNMENT

The Bible mentions a man named Nimrod, who built a number of large cities. Genesis 10:10 refers to "the first centers of his kingdom," so apparently he ruled these cities as well.

We have all seen the movies with monarchs. There are the good, benevolent monarchs who rule well with their absolute power over others. We have also seen the movies with the horrible, selfish monarchs who were cruel or evil in using their absolute power over others. The books of world history are full of examples of good and not-so-good monarchs.

Monarchs can also be female. They can also be kind or cruel. They also have absolute authority over their subjects and disobeying can mean severe punishment or death. Many times countries were run by queens instead of kings. History is full of good and bad examples of female monarchs as well.

Here is the big idea in a monarchy: one person has more authority than the other spouse and makes all decisions. His or her voice alone is the *ultimate* authority. The monarch has to the right to punish his subjects if they don't obey him.

In a monarchy, the decision structure is simple: ask the king or queen. Whatever this person says, regardless of how sensible, biblical, or sane the decision is, all others in the family will comply. In terms of Nimrod's rule,

remember that this was the first government of men trying to rule themselves. Also note that God did not establish Nimrod as a ruler over others. Nimrod established
himself, or others did. This first-time government was
man's idea.

A friend of mine came to one of my marriage conferences. After the conference we went out to eat. As we
were walking, my friend stopped me and said, "Doug,
I think I'm really a democracy form of government except when I buy cars—then I am a total monarchy." He
would go buy cars without any consideration of what
his wife thought! He asked if it's possible to be a part-
time monarch.

THE SECOND-IN-TIME GOVERNMENT

The next form of government was a theocracy. This
government was established after the children of Israel
left Egypt. Egypt itself was a true monarchy; Pharaoh
was thought to be a god (these are always the worst
monarchs).

A theocracy is basically a group of equals trying to
discern God's will on a matter. In a marital theocracy,
God is the ultimate Ruler of both the husband and wife.
The husband and wife are equal and both can hear from
God. The goal of a theocracy is to obey God and not
each other, regardless of gender. Practically speaking,
only very mature and secure people can operate a theocracy in marriage.

Sad to say, theocracy probably had the shortest run
in history of any form of government. It wasn't long before the Israelites wanted a king like the other nations.

You remember how the Israelites asked Samuel for a king and God gave them King Saul (1 Sam. 9), then David, and many other kings after that.

Monarchy became the government in Israel and throughout the world. It would be many years until the next form of government would be born.

THE THIRD-IN-TIME GOVERNMENT

In 1776, a new government was born. After the bloodshed of many men on both sides of the war, America won its independence from England. The leaders of this great new nation formed a government with no trace of a monarchy.

They established a government "by the people and for the people." This government presumed that all people had equal rights given by their Creator. People were free to create their own futures. This government had a unique system of checks and balances to protect the people from ever being overrun by those who led them.

This government included the right to vote, which included the duty to choose the best person to lead the people. In this way majority, not an individual, ruled.

As Americans, we know that the system isn't perfect. And it's true that in a marriage this form of government has strengths and weaknesses. One of the strengths of a democracy is that it presumes equality: husband and wife are equal and their ideas are equal. A practical weakness is that both people have to agree to come to a final decision. If, then, we are voting on what gets planted in the garden, as Frank and Anna might, it could be years before anything gets done.

As democracy moved along, there came another form of government that developed through the Industrial Revolution.

THE FOURTH-IN-TIME GOVERNMENT

As time clicked on, America grew. She found herself birthing large companies. These companies began to create their own structures to govern themselves. I want to look at a valuable power configuration in a corporation that we will call the *vice-presidential structure*.

At the top of any given corporation is a president—the final authoritative word. He is usually served by vice presidents. Vice presidents have very specific areas of responsibility. In a given corporation you have the vice president of marketing, the vice president of sales, and the vice president of finances. The vice presidents are equals but have entirely different functions.

In their areas of specialty, the vice presidents have 100 percent authority. They can consult other vice presidents but do as they wish in their spheres of influence.

Now, how does this apply to a marriage? In your marriage, you and your spouse are vice presidents—God is your President. Areas of responsibility are divided. Vice President A might have the various responsibilities of the cars, garage, garden, housecleaning (some), and plumbing. Vice President B might take care of dry cleaning, housecleaning (some), bill paying, and house service calls. Both vice presidents would share or divide various financial, children, pet, and extended family responsibilities as well.

Establishing task distribution can save you many

long arguments and help you benefit from the Ten-Minute Marriage Principle. If you choose to operate in a vice presidential structure, you'll both be clear on who is responsible for what. Clarity in a marriage is very helpful! Then one spouse can make a decision regarding his/her area of responsibility without disrespecting the other spouse. You and your spouse can enjoy each other's support.

Suppose Nancy has the responsibility of the garden. She wants to plant tomatoes. She consults Bill, her husband, and he thinks spinach might be a good idea. Nancy can do anything she wants: plant all tomatoes, some tomatoes and some spinach, all spinach, or something totally different. She is the vice president; she has authority over the garden to do as she pleases.

Whatever Nancy chooses, Bill's feelings aren't hurt. Why? Because they created a vice-presidential structure and he knows he is only a consultant in regards to the garden. Bill also knows, when he asks Nancy to consult on the garage, he still can do as he feels right. Both respect each other as people and as vice presidents with authority over certain domains.

On some issues, however, the vice presidents must work together to achieve their company's success. They meet to discuss bigger questions in which they have equal say, such as neighborhoods to live in, churches, children, education, retirement, and spending. Since a group or board of this type operates as a democracy, you would both have to agree for a decision to pass. As a two-member board, you both must say yes before the "bill" can be "passed."

Some couples actually create a three-member board.

This third member can be a spiritual leader like a pastor, elder, or spiritually mature couple. The third member of the board can be permanent or situational. You might have an accountant, tax advisor, doctor, or other specialist as a temporary board member for different important decisions. The third board member has the controlling vote.

It would work like this: you and your spouse are locked on a decision for a considerable time and you need to reach a decision. You both present your cases calmly and factually to your board member, he or she votes, and that is the end of the conversation.

If you choose a third board member, make sure that person is spiritually grounded, fair-minded, and not easily moved by emotional presentations. Having an extended board member can help you maintain more of the Ten-Minute Marriage Principle because you won't waste time fussing for months about a decision. You can spend more time building up your relationship instead!

If you choose a vice-presidential structure of government, decide if you will have a two- or three-member board. Regardless, I strongly recommend you both consult the President—the Lord Jesus Christ—to guide you and your board. After all, He always makes the right decisions.

LET'S REVIEW

Here is a summary of the various governments that we have discussed. You can concisely view these options and decide what form you would like to adopt so you know how decisions are to be made in your marriage.

Monarchy

- One person is superior and makes decisions.
- One person follows the decision made by the superior.

Theocracy

- Each person is equal.
- Both seek and hear God.
- Both follow what God is telling them.

Democracy

- Each person is equal.
- Ideas are debated and voted upon.
- Both follow the direction of the vote.

Vice-Presidential Structure

- Each vice president is equal with a different and clearly defined area of responsibility.
- Sometimes VPs add a third member to their board.
- Both follow the decision of the third person. All consult the President (Jesus)!

I love this part of the process of creating a new government. Regardless of the government you had in the past, you can create any form of government you choose. As with any nation that gets to choose a new government, any option is legitimate. Remember that, unless you choose a monarchy, the government structure is stronger than you or your wishes.

One year Lisa and I used our government process to make a mutual decision to get debt-free. That year I saw three new cars I wanted to purchase, but I couldn't because as a government we had made a decision, and that decision was greater than my desires or me.

Maybe you have come up with some combinations of governments you would like to try for a while. That's fine; you can be as creative as you want. It's best, though, to write down what kind of government you establish. You can refer to this later if a question comes up about who has say over what.

Let us see how each of you would like to make decisions. On the following pages are places for his vote, her vote, and a final vote. For the moment, we are going to suspend any previous governments you may have had. For this exercise, both persons in the marriage are totally equal. You can now create a government that reflects the true desires of each spouse—that is, once you come to an agreement.

Remember that God is a God of order, not chaos. He can use whatever government you choose. But not choosing one can leave you and your marriage in a state of indefinite disorder.

His Vote

- ☐ Monarchy (Husband as king)
- ☐ Monarchy (Wife as queen)
- ☐ Theocracy
- ☐ Democracy
- ☐ Vice President
- ☐ Other _____

Her Vote

- ☐ Monarchy (Husband as king)
- ☐ Monarchy (Wife as queen)
- ☐ Theocracy
- ☐ Democracy
- ☐ Vice President
- ☐ Other _____

I realize you might have some differences and need to discuss this for a while. That's fine. But if you get deadlocked, go see a pastor, counselor, or spiritually mature couple to help you resolve this.

FINAL VOTE

☐ Monarchy (Husband as king)
☐ Monarchy (Wife as queen)
☐ Theocracy
☐ Democracy
☐ Vice President
☐ Other _____

Here is a way you can solidify your efforts today. After every new government is created, there is always paperwork. But we will make it short. Take out a piece of paper and write:

We, Mr._____ and Mrs. _____ hereby declare our government to be _____ _____.

Signed _____ Date _____

Signed _____ Date _____

Congratulations! You have just completed your new government! You can shake hands and pose for the photographers if you wish. Seriously, though, this one decision can make a very large difference in the way you relate to one another, function around each other, and ultimately the way you respect each other as adults. A government allows respect to fill your marriage in a new, life-giving manner.

I wish you the absolute best as you hold hands lovingly and respectfully and you face the many decisions in life. With a government in place, you have a spelled-out process by which to make decisions and settle conflicts. You deserve the peace and calm of a stable government.

Like Charlie, who now knows where his keys are, you now know how decisions are made in your marriage. This support principle of government will allow you much more time for connecting. These support principles help your Ten-Minute Marriage Principle stay strong.

Remember that if you work your core muscles and your extended muscle groups, you will have a whole body that is stronger and even looks better. In this support principle of government, you have tackled a big idea that can add vigor to your marriage, as you stay consistent with your core.

As you know, there are more support principles that go into making a marriage vibrant with health. So keep turning the pages!

5

THE EXTERNALLY
MOTIVATED MATE

I love being a counselor. Every day I have the opportunity to meet people from all walks of life. I have found out many things about people that I didn't learn in college, including all kinds of discoveries about how men and women think and feel. One of these I want to share with you in this chapter: how men and women are motivated and how that can affect your living the Ten-Minute Marriage Principle.

As a spouse, you know that God created marriage to be a real education in itself! As spouses grow together over time, each learns about the other: what he likes to do, what she likes to eat, how he takes care of himself, how she manages her time, how he likes his coffee or tea, how she likes or doesn't like certain family members. You learn how hard your spouse works or how hard he or she avoids certain tasks. Learning about your spouse is definitely a lifelong journey. I actually am amazed at how much I still learn about Lisa even after being married to her for more than twenty years.

In these pages I want to show you a very important aspect of understanding yourself and your spouse. When you have more insight into how both of you are motivated, you can avoid many conflicts and misunderstandings. This alone can be one of the variables to help you to practice more successfully the Ten-Minute Marriage Principle.

You see, understanding how someone is motivated can help you navigate life decisions and relationships. If you have insight into how your spouse values different things or is hurt by certain things, then you can learn how to better support your spouse.

Once you understand how your spouse is motivated, you can really understand the value he or she has as a person in your life. You can relax, stop trying to change him or her. Your spouse's motivational DNA is something that can give you practical ideas for making your marriage a smoother experience for both of you.

This idea of understanding your spouse and his or her motivational DNA strengthens your choice to live the Ten-Minute Marriage Principle. If you work this muscle appropriately, you will learn to cooperate with, instead of fight against, how God made you and your spouse uniquely for each other. The exercises will be easier to complete because you'll feel safe and understood by your partner. You will gain a deeper appreciation for each other and for God's bringing you together.

TWO COUPLES, ONE CONFLICT

Maria and Martin were a couple who benefited by understanding each other's motivation. When I met them, Maria and Martin were actually separated due to Martin's infidelity. Maria was a vivacious, red-haired, fifty-year-old woman who looked about thirty-five. She was physically active and had started her own company years before. She handled the marketing, staffing, and running of her fairly successful company. Maria was not only full of life, she was full of ideas. Once this company was making enough income, she invested in some real estate and was doing rather well with this venture as well. To meet Maria was to meet a modern-day Proverbs 31 woman. She was godly to the bone and loved her husband, family, and church.

During their visit to our counseling center, we discovered a major issue that Maria had had with Martin for years. To her, he was always a "tagalong." He seemed to lack initiative. Frequently throughout their marriage Martin worked for Maria. He was responsible, on time, and a friendly Christian man. But Maria wanted Martin to "make it on his own" before she reconciled with him. She wanted him to wake up full of ambition and not be able to rest because of all the ideas he had to improve things and create wealth for their family.

Maria's hidden heart's desire was that Martin would become just like her. She had many judgments about Martin and who he really was. Once she was able to understand how they were created differently in terms of motivation, she was able to let go of her expectations and criticisms and begin to accept the strengths of Martin's motivation.

Victor and Elaine were another couple who really didn't understand each other's motivation. Victor's family were immigrants and they worked hard to start a company in real estate. Victor inherited the company at a young age due to his parents' early death. Elaine grew up middle-class, went to college, and worked at a government agency before working with Victor. Victor was a large man and had a commanding presence. Elaine was sweet, friendly, and petite, and she usually didn't talk much unless you asked her direct questions. She was, however, a godly woman full of wisdom when she did speak.

Victor grew his parents' modest company into a large, recognized commercial real estate company in a several-city region. Victor was up early and worked hard, and he loved to give to the down-and-out and ministries that helped truly disadvantaged people around the world.

Victor was usually full of ideas. But he felt really constrained by Elaine because she questioned his decisions. She called it "helping," but Victor found it annoying. Victor was quick to download his success in his ventures. He wasn't as quick to talk about the bankruptcy of ten years ago or the near-bankruptcy of three years ago. Both of these occurred after Victor made a deal with people Elaine cautioned him about.

Victor was really frustrated with Elaine and sought counseling. Overall they had a pretty good marriage and family. They dated weekly, prayed regularly, were involved in the children's lives, and had mutual interests. They also had good relationships with their pastor and church. They had learned to live within their means and both liked to hike behind their house a few times a week. Elaine handled the details both at home and the office. She made the closings and leasing of property happen and felt secure in her gifting as part of their business together.

Although Victor and Elaine's marriage was relatively in good shape, their understanding of each other was not. Victor and Elaine's fights were like the clash of the Titans. Victor pitted his large person and personality along with a huge rage up against this sweet, quiet, stubborn woman, and they had long fights. Elaine held her own: she didn't attack, but she wouldn't give up either.

This clashing would sometimes last days and, depending on Victor's ability to manage his emotions, could impact the marriage and family for days or weeks. Once, however, they each learned how the other was motivated, they were able to respect each other and move through conflict much more easily.

Maria and Martin and Victor and Elaine were all able to let go of some misunderstandings and judgments. If you explore this idea of motivation, you also might enjoy a stronger marriage and better appreciate God's wisdom in giving you the gift of each other.

TWO TYPES OF MOTIVATION

Here is a paradigm for understanding motivation that has helped couples like those we've have just been looking at. People are motivated *internally* or *externally*, and this affects how they think about, view, decide, and manage everything in life.

Let me explain this in a parental analogy you will probably relate to. Let's talk about the age-old request that your child go clean his or her room. If you have an externally motivated child, you breathe easy as he responds, "Okay." You go back to your chores and, for the most part, you are confident that this child is cleaning his room. The actual level of cleanliness might not be up to your adult standards, but you can tell the child made a legitimate attempt.

Now you go to your next child. You use the same calm voice as you tell her to clean her room. This child is internally motivated, so she did not come up with the idea, and to her the idea is suspect. She begins to question: "Why do I need to clean my room? It's not dirty. I just cleaned it last week. I'm really busy doing this—I will do that later."

Then you gently suggest your idea again: "Go clean your room."

Now the internally motivated child is starting to feel controlled, ordered, and disrespected (because you're not listening to her valid ideas). So she responds more harshly to your second request: "I don't want to clean my room right now." If she concedes to going to her room, she will start reading a book, move about like a turtle, slam things around, or use other ways to punish you for not respecting her personhood.

You as the parent know you are going to have to check on her progress. You may actually have to station yourself in the room to validate any progress at all. You can begin to get angry, rude, and threaten her, but your emotional reaction seems to have little impact on this child.

As a parent you want to compare the two children: "Why can't you listen like your externally motivated sibling?" Even if you don't say it, you are probably asking yourself why one child is so different from another.

Let me use another parenting analogy that actually happened in our home. Like many of you, I have one externally motivated and one internally motivated child.

This conflict happened around the ever-popular issue of getting homework completed. My externally motivated child had no problem getting homework done. It was perfectly fine for someone to suggest it to him and for him to do it. This wasn't so true of my internally motivated daughter. When Hadassah was in second grade, her homework consisted of some spelling words and some math.

For many weeks Lisa would spend hours a night with Hadassah doing this homework that should have taken less than half an hour. Lisa liked doing the homework with Hadassah and often declined my help in this area. But finally, one night Lisa was at her wits' end. She called me upstairs to our bedroom and said, "You have to help her with her homework. I can't handle one more night." Lisa looked so overwhelmed and desperate that of course I agreed.

I went downstairs. About twenty minutes later, I came bopping up the steps.

Lisa asked, "What are you doing up here? She needs to finish her homework."

"She's finished," I replied.

"No way!" Lisa exclaimed.

"She is finished. You can go check," I said.

Lisa shot out of the bedroom like a wild animal on the hunt. She grabbed the homework papers that were still on the table and to her amazement saw that it was true. With a tone of mixed surprise and disbelief, she asked, "How did you do that?"

I said, "You have been trying to get her to do homework because it's the right thing to do and because she should care about it. I happen to know that she is internally motivated, so she feels disrespected and controlled by this constrained system. So I had to make it her idea to want to do the homework. Once it was her idea, she applied her resources to finishing her homework instead of depleting my resources."

Lisa, intrigued, questioned further, "What do you mean?"

"It's simple. I placed a quarter in front of Hadassah [who likes having her own money to spend and give away] and told her if she was done in thirty minutes, she could have the quarter. If not, I would keep the quarter. Then she wanted the quarter [her idea] and had to do homework as a way to reach *her own* goal [she felt respected]."

Lisa smiled. She began to apply the internally motivated principle in her parenting and, all of a sudden, homework became much easier in our house.

Why did I start with child analogies? First, because kids can have the same environment, gene pool, and similar experiences but still be extremely different in motivation. Also, I wanted to emphasize that judging one style of motivation as better or more desirable is not a good idea. Both of my children are great. They are smart, disciplined, and godly, and I love them both dearly. Yet when it comes to motivation, they are extremely different. *Different is good*. Although one may require more parental creativity than the other, God has an incredible plan for them both.

People often marry people of the opposite motivation. The trick is not to value yours as the better or more godly way. In Christ you are absolutely different and absolutely equal. When we look at our motivation as a way to be superior to anyone, we sin.

In this chapter I will focus on externally motivated people (whom I will call EMs) and look at internally motivated people (IMs) in the next chapter.

Characteristics of an Externally Motivated Person

Each person's motivational style has strengths and weaknesses. Of course the strengths of the externally motivated can be perceived as weaknesses by internally motivated people and vice versa. To avoid the strengths/weaknesses pitfalls, I want to describe some characteristics of the externally motivated individual. If many of these fit you or your spouse, you can better understand, appreciate, and love your spouse and how he or she is designed. I hope, too, that this explanation will relieve you of wanting your spouse to become just like you as well!

RULES HAVE VALUE

EMs place a high value on rules, laws, and other guidelines in life. They value that others have spent time, for example, evaluating how fast cars should go. They understand that there is probably a good reason for these ideas. They don't need to validate the research, they just believe that the rules are probably a good idea and we would all do better in life if we follow them.

This means if someone is getting off an exit ramp and the ramp speed is thirty-five miles per hour, generally an EM would drive thirty-five miles per hour. There is no real need to go past the speed limit even if his or her spouse doesn't value the rules in the same way.

RIGHT AND WRONG ARE PERMANENT

EMs seem to have a heightened sense of right and wrong. Right is always right and wrong is always wrong. They don't have much room for fudging, and the idea of there being shades in between is only nonsense. EMs' moral development, under normal conditions, is pretty good. They generally believe right is always right no matter who you are, how much money you make, where you live, what you drive, who you know, no matter what time of day or what country you are in or who is around to watch you. This strong moral compass is a gift that most externally motivated people I have met possess.

FOLLOWING DIRECTIONS

EMs have little difficulty following reasonable directions. It's totally acceptable for others to have ideas.

EMs don't take others' ideas as some personal attack. Generally they will follow the directions given by a person in authority without much question or grievance. EMs also have their own ideas and if they believe they have a better solution, they suggest it without necessarily seeing this as questioning authority.

IDEA DETACHMENT

EMs seem to have an ability to separate their ideas from who they are. If their idea is better than another person's, they don't see themselves as superior—even if the person is a boss. They do not think of ideas as bad, good, smart, or less than smart.

EMs generally have the ability to say "Okay" and go with the flow if their ideas aren't the best solutions. This detachment from their ideas allows them to cooperate and be team players with much less pettiness and competition than their internally motivated counterparts at home or at the office.

MANAGES WELL

There are exceptions to this, but most of the externally motivated people I have met seem to manage things well. They have a good general sense of organization in their lives. They know how to complete tasks in an efficient manner. If they are managing a store, shop, home, or Fortune 500 company, or if they are secretaries or administrative assistants, things are getting done. EMs value being dependable and efficient. Generally speaking, in my experience, when you delegate responsibility to externally motivated people, you can be assured that the responsibility will be handled well.

I travel a lot and speak at conferences both nationally and internationally, and I can always tell when externally motivated people are running things. I always feel cared for and it's clear someone has thought ahead about what I might need. I can relax the whole time I am at the conference.

CONSCIENTIOUS

Conscientiousness is another of the characteristics of EMs. IMs are also conscientious, but my experience is that the externally motivated person has a heightened sense of this trait.

EMs care about the primary people in their lives. They care how others are doing. They have a way of getting into other people's worlds and feeling what those people feel.

They pay attention to what they are doing because the quality of their work is a reflection on them. Their work and their responses in a relationship matter quite a bit. They may think about a small comment they made and wonder if they hurt someone's feelings. EMs actually lose sleep over such an incident. If they feel they could do better on a project, for themselves or for others, staying up late to finish is somehow mandatory.

This conscientiousness is a gift. Somehow externally motivated people *are* their work and relationships; failure there, whether real or perceived, is taken very seriously. This depth of feeling isn't really changeable—it's hardwired into them.

THOROUGH PROCESSING

When faced with a decision or asked about their opinion on a matter of importance, EMs need a significant amount of time to process information. This is connected to caring and being conscientious. These people think though all the various angles and relational impacts of the decision or opinion they are being asked about.

To EMs, a quick opinion or decision is suspect. They doubt the sincerity or validity of the instant decisions that others propose.

My experience has showed that if I want EMs to feel comfortable with a decision, I have to discuss it with them on one day, give them time to think about it for another day or so, then schedule a time to discuss their thoughts on the matter.

If you pressure EMs, you will frustrate them. They know they can't possibly think of all the ramifications in a few minutes. If rushed into a decision, they feel guilty because they didn't do their best on the issue. They can't accept less than a thorough processing of decisions and important opinions. Because of this, EMs experience stress with decisions. Don't expect that they will ever face decisions lightheartedly or make them quickly.

This must be appreciated, not undervalued or perceived as a weakness. These people are not putting off deciding, they are actually thinking everything through, so patience and some extra time are important to respect EMs' makeup.

DILIGENCE WITH DETAILS

For some people, details are burdens. For EMs, they are an acceptable and valuable part of life. You see, to them, details help others to live life well, do things better, and reach heights that otherwise could never be achieved.

EMs are often the unspoken, unseen heroes in life. In a play, the audience acknowledges and praises the actors. But for every actor there is one or more people specializing in the details: the seamstresses for all the costumes who never spoke a line, the light person who doesn't ask for praise, the sound people who worked flawlessly, the stage crew who pulled this, carried that, and made the scene transitions as unnoticeable as possible.

So it is with the externally motivated. They are the people who make possible the quality of life others enjoy. They are the wind many others are able to fly upon.

SEEING THE POSSIBLE CONSEQUENCES

Here is a gift that people can too often misunderstand or undervalue. EMs can see not only what's possible but what can possibly go wrong. They can see why an idea might not be flawless.

EMs can also see why people won't buy this object or idea, why a commercial won't work, why doing this or that could be shortsighted. This can be frustrating for those whose ideas are "flawless" from conception (internally motivated people)! But this gift is part of the process of making good decisions. They see the problems so they can be fixed or addressed prior to implementation. This thinking prevents the embarrassment of bad consequences. EMs think it is better to bang your head at the idea stage than at the reality stage.

If you are married to an EM, thank God. He or she can be your—and your idea's—best friend. Once you go through and rebuild the idea with the adequate modification to rectify negative consequences, your idea has a much better chance of a long life.

CONFLICT IS NOT ENJOYABLE

EMs do not enjoy conflict. They do not enjoy battles in a marriage. They need time to process, so often conflict doesn't provide the time they need to be their best. They are often not great at thinking on their feet. They would rather take time to think it through than see how fast a conflict can be resolved.

They feel they should solve an issue not quickly but rightly. If you are married to an EM, you must look at conflict in a different way. If you use conflict to manipulate or emotionally overpower your spouse, you will exacerbate the situation. Now you are multiplying the pressure on the externally motivated person.

It's as if conflict itself already adds a hundred pounds of pressure, and then the insanity of manipulation and emotional bullying makes it a thousand pounds of pressure. EMs have to push back with great intensity just to stop the pressure or to be heard.

If this has been your approach with your externally motivated spouse, you are the one loading the cannon, putting the gunpowder in, and lighting it. When your spouse seems to become overly stressed in response, this should indicate to you that you need to use a different strategy to truly resolve a conflict.

DOING THE RIGHT THING

A last characteristic of EMs is that they feel really good when they do the right thing. Now, this is probably true of all of us, but it is heightened in the externally motivated.

Remember how I mentioned that right and wrong are permanent for EMs? Well, for such people to feel congruent, they must do what they know is correct and true. If you ask a spouse who is externally motivated to lie or cheat, he or she will feel so awful it can mess him or her up for years.

To do wrong for any reason creates such pain for an EM that it is almost traumatic. Such actions are against his or her entire person. For the externally motivated, doing the right thing is not an idea, it is who they are. The externally motivated deserve to do the good that is in them. Never ask them to do wrong or intentionally cause pain for others.

This is not changeable, nor are these people being sissies, Pollyannas, or do-gooders. To attack them as if they were just adds insult to injury. They can no more change this characteristic than they can change their height.

SELAH

We have covered much information so far but, as we say in Colorado, we are not at the top of the mountain yet. We who climb mountains also know the importance of taking a break before we continue to climb.

Let's review before we move to the next chapter. Externally motivated people:

- Believe rules have value.
- Believe right and wrong are permanent.
- Find it easy to follow directions.
- Can separate themselves from their ideas.
- Manage well.
- Are conscientious.
- Process thoroughly.
- Are diligent with details.
- See the possible consequences of a decision.
- Do not enjoy conflict.
- Need to do the right thing.

Have you discovered anything—or have you connected with any of the information you just read? Have you found out that your spouse is an EM? If so, in the past you may have thought that some of the strengths of EMs were weaknesses or personality quirks. You may have also hoped that some of these characteristics could somehow be changed. I hope this chapter helps you accept your spouse for who he or she is: a precious gift from God to others to help you better do life.

If this chapter has been revelatory for you, write

down what you have learned and how you will change your attitudes and actions because of it. How will your marriage be different now that you know how an EM is hardwired?

You may have also learned that you are an EM. If so, you must value the way God created you. You may need to learn how to maintain boundaries, especially when it comes to processing or making decisions; you will need to ask for the time you need to "think it through." You also need to realize that although you might have innate gifts due to your motivation, your spouse may not have the same core motivation as you—but his or her way is just as valuable. You will find many applications to your motivation in your marriage and other relationships. What I hope you learn in this chapter and the next, more than anything, are appreciation and respect for your spouse if he or she is externally motivated.

With knowledge comes responsibility. I know today much better how my Lisa is made, therefore I am responsible to respect, appreciate, and not try to change her. She was wonderful when I dated her and is more wonderful twenty years later. Be encouraged that understanding your spouse's motivation can lead to greater peace in your marriage—which in turn will help both of you uphold the Ten-Minute Marriage Principle.

How? As you add this support principle of understanding your spouse's motivation to practicing the daily Ten-Minute Marriage Principle, you will begin empowering your relationship. You'll face less conflict and enjoy more camaraderie. You'll be more willing to invest in your relationship by doing the exercises.

As I mentioned earlier in the chapter, there are two

motivational paradigms. We have touched on the externally motivated in this chapter. If you haven't found yourself or your spouse yet, just turn the page. You may learn quite a bit about yourself or the person you married.

Keep reading, learning, and loving each other!

6

THE INTERNALLY
MOTIVATED MATE

This is going to be an interesting topic, so strap in for further understanding of yourself or your spouse. Next I'm going to describe the characteristics I have seen in the internally motivated person (IM). Although you or your spouse might not have 100 percent of the listed qualities, you will see a definite pattern for the internally motivated soul. Remember that they, like the externally motivated, come hardwired this way from God as a gift to you and others.

Again, as you add your understanding of your spouse's motivation to daily practice of the Ten-Minute Marriage Principle, you will enrich the fitness of your marriage. So let's dig right in!

The primary motivation for IMs comes totally from within themselves. The genesis for motivation is not environment or relationships, but how IMs themselves think, feel, perceive, and evaluate a system from within.

IMs might be wrongly perceived as totally selfish. They tend to approach things this way: if it's not their idea or their way of doing things, there is no other way. In truth, IMs have been created to mostly rely upon their own perceptions or ideas as truth or reality. You see, they have already thought about how things should go and made conclusions before the discussion occurs. So when they push for their own ideas, they are not being stubborn or mean-spirited, they just have already figured it out internally.

Remember my daughter, who fought against doing her homework until I made it her idea to get it done so she could earn a quarter? This is an IM; she has to create or buy into an idea and make it her own to be motivated. Although IMs can mature enough to hear and value others, their ideas are really the standard in their minds.

The gift of the IMs is that often they will lead and be persistent in finishing their ideas. We will see, as we look further, that this motivational style is truly a gift just like external motivation.

Let me tell you a quick story of an IM who was married to another internally motivated person. (These couples are the funnest to work with because they believe all their ideas are good or even the best ideas. This makes for some pretty lively counseling sessions, to say the least.) The wife was explaining how mad she gets around Christmastime because of all that's expected of her: she has to go gift shopping, decorate, entertain, and attend parties. As we continued to talk, it became very obvious that Christmas wasn't bothering her; it was all the related activities—and the fact that these activities were not her idea—that caused the problem. She resented that she had to do all that work.

Once she was able to see this, she was able to make progress on developing her Christmas spirit. She had to allow others (including God) to have valid ideas she could go along with. She didn't need to resent holiday activities; she needed only to accept that these activities were good things worth her time and energy.

Again, outside ideas are truly suspect to IMs. Accepting other people's ideas can mean to the IM that he or she is inadequate or stupid. I know it doesn't sound logical (especially to externally motivated people, to whom ideas are impersonal and equal in value), but it's not about logic, it's about perception. This is how they really feel and think. Much like externally motivated persons, IMs' ideas are who they are.

For example, to offend an EM you would criticize the job he or she does. To offend an IM, you would criticize his or her ideas. For EMs, they do, therefore they are. For IMs, they think, therefore they are.

CHARACTERISTICS OF THE INTERNALLY MOTIVATED

OUTSIDE-THE-BOX THINKING

IMs hold such things as rules, guidelines, and laws lightly. You see, all of these are actually other people's ideas, so they are suspect until "purchased" by the IM. While EMs see these ideas as valid and worthy of obedience, IMs do not.

Because IMs hold such ideas so lightly, they feel free to ask questions: Why is this guideline here? Who thought of this? How long ago? Is there a better idea? Should we consider change?

Once the questions begin, any answer is really an option. IMs can generate many possible options. They will come up with these ideas without considering moral values, the impact on others, or how realistic the ideas actually are. The process of brainstorming is a deep delight to IMs.

To ask IMs to solve a problem or create a new idea is like asking them to take a motorcycle ride in the mountains. It makes them so happy, they can almost feel the wind caress their faces. They feel trusted and significant when they are asked to come up with ideas.

I know this doesn't make sense to the externally motivated person. Remember that both internally and externally motivated people are gifts, and they don't have to totally change to be successful in marriage. They just need to mature and accept each other.

PRONE TO RELATIVE THINKING

IMs are more prone to relative thinking than their external counterparts. Right, wrong, truth, and even facts can initially all be ignored when IMs are creating ideas. This is especially true if they are pursuing something they really want or really want to do.

Their internal impulses often lead IMs. I dated a very godly woman in Bible school. She gave me a gift of insight about myself: "Doug, you think you're really a man of your mind. Really you are a man of your heart, and you use your mind to justify what your heart wants."

I wasn't wise enough to understand what all those words meant, but over time I have grown to appreciate them. What she was saying was, "Doug, once you decide something in your heart, you mind creates all kinds of reasons, plans, schemes, and angles to get or achieve something." (Yes, I am internally motivated.)

This means that I can justify relative thinking because it's a means to an end. I see this in my office all the time with IM clients who have not morally matured in their thinking. What I mean by this is they have not accepted the absolutes of Scripture about lying and stealing. They can rationalize not paying a bill in order to buy a toy they want. They can rationalize not giving all the information to someone if the person didn't ask the exact right question.

If you are an EM, this could wear you out because you feel as if you have to be a lawyer to get the truth from IMs.

It's true at times that these people are flat-out lying. Mature IMs learn the difference between when they are creatively thinking and lying. Relative thinking can be a gift when creating solutions or approaches to accomplishing something. The relativity allows suspension of ideas that are already accepted or conventional wisdom. Aren't we happy for the person who thought outside of the box and dreamed up communicating without wires?

Under the direction of the Holy Spirit, this trait can be a blessing and blast to those around them.

OVERESTIMATE THEIR OWN IDEAS

IMs tend to overestimate their own ideas. If you are married to an IM and you challenge his or her idea without respect, you could be in a battle that you'll lose even if you are right. This is because of IMs' persistence, lack of rules, multiple angles on an idea, and the speed at which they throw their idea punches.

You can't change that they respect their ideas, so work with it. Understand even if they put only a fraction of a second of thought into something—to them the thought itself has value. The fact that it went through the processor of their brains or hearts gives this thought value.

As a spouse you can spend hours fighting with IMs about things they may not highly value, such as right, wrong, or tradition, or you can utilize their respect for their ideas. Ask them, "How did you get to that conclusion? What would you think about this option? How do you think this person might feel about this or react to it?" IMs almost always interpret being asked questions as respectful, not burdensome. *Ask permission* to co-create with an IM to or allow others to co-create with him or her—don't presume this will be okay. I know this takes more time and effort than just blasting their obviously less-than-thought-through ideas, but it can save your marriage some wear and tear.

Let me give you a very common problem for the IM. It's Saturday morning and the IM has just awakened. Before very long this person has an idea (remember, ideas are valuable) of how the day should go. He or she puts together in some order the household tasks, errands, kids' activities, fun things to do, and where dinner might take place.

This all happens without his or her consulting you about changes that occurred with the kids' events and other errands that the IM didn't think of. You can fight about the day, or you can learn to consult each other the night before. Make an agreement to co-create a day; then the IM has brought ideas into the plan, and you will have his or her resources working *with* the plan instead of *against* it all day long.

SPEEDY DECISIONS ARE BEST

Here is one of the big contrasts between the internally and externally motivated: EMs value the thoroughness of a decision—did they think through it enough, consider relationships, consequences, and other future ramifications? IMs value the speed at which they make a decision. Hypothetically collecting data, assimilating it, creating solutions, and moving forward quickly are of great value to the internally motivated. Again, this can drive an EM crazy because of the contrast in values.

Again, though, this speedy processing is a gift. You want your surgeon, police officer, firefighter, military men and women, and many others to be able to make fast, accurate decisions. IMs welcome questions from EMs, so asking for the slower version—"How did you come up with that?"—is okay. Sometimes you will be impressed with all that went into that quick decision; other times you won't. Regardless, understanding that speed has value for IMs is critical to understanding and living with them.

IMs like to see decisions made. If they are the ones deciding, they would like to do so quickly and move on to the next things in their lives. Most decisions are not difficult for IMs; in most cases they would rather make *any* decision than wait for days to make the "right" decision.

If IMs have not matured enough to accept others and instead think that everyone should be like them, they will not honor the time value of EMs. They will see processing as a waste of time, whether they're deciding on something with long-term impact or just where to go for dinner.

If, for example, you are married to an IM husband, and he gives you the responsibility of making a decision, ask how much time you have to make that decision. Ask if you are ultimately deciding or if you are co-deciding. If you are going out together, for example, ask if you are making or joining in making the decision, then ask how long—say, until the babysitter arrives?—you have to do it. Then both of you will be less frustrated. You'll both enjoy the date because your IM husband feels relaxed that a decision has been made, and you'll feel more relaxed having weighed in on that decision.

This is an interesting difference between the internally and externally motivated: EMs find decision making stressful; IMs love it! They want to decide and move on, so they get fidgety if you delay. Therefore, if you are an EM and you want to talk about moving or a vacation, come prepared to the conversation. Spend some time thinking through your ideas before actually bringing them up with your IM spouse. This will save you both some stress.

CONSEQUENCES AREN'T IMPORTANT

Although speed in thinking and deciding is valuable to IMs, perceiving consequences often is not one of their skills. Here an IM could really utilize the strength of an EM in marriage, life, or business.

The "what could possibly go wrong" thought is not usually as strong as the "of course this can work" thought for IMs. The IMs, left to themselves, could come up with lots of ideas, spend lots of time and money on developing these ideas, and not learn why people don't like their idea until the end of the project. IMs are usually optimistic and persistent, but they don't often visualize the consequences.

If you have, for example, an IM wife, you can encourage her idea but help her utilize her creative brain to foresee consequences. Gently say, "I think this idea has value, but do me a favor: can you think of five or ten reasons why it wouldn't work so we can address these on the front end?" Help her come up with these ideas. She will probably also come up with solutions, so be sincere in helping and don't just try to squash her idea.

When an EM and an IM work together, the idea has a much better chance of surviving. The two, balancing each other with respect, can make most decisions wisely.

CONFLICT ISN'T BAD

IMs accept conflicts as part of the process of life. It isn't something they need to avoid. Ultimately conflict is good because it means getting or going somewhere, and even better if it leads ultimately to a conclusion.

It's not necessarily the intent of IMs to start conflict, but rarely will they back down. It's not because they are egotistical maniacs. They believe in their ideas—remember, their ideas are who they are.

Therefore, if you strongly disagree, be prepared to face conflict. IMs don't mind engaging in conflict because it lets them use their strengths. They enjoy thinking fast, pulling facts, history, knowledge of their opponent, persistence, and energy into something.

Conflict is like revving a powerful engine to IMs. They maneuver well in conflict, and they sometimes enjoy the strategy or test to see how fully convinced you are of your ideas. Mature IMs handle conflict more respectfully and hopefully with the goal of doing God's will, not always their own. If you are married to an IM, it's important to choose which battles you want to fight and to have thought though several points before you go into conflict. This way you co-create solutions without having to win or lose.

Always be clear in a conflict with an IM as to what the real objective is. Is the objective a win-win solution, just having fun arguing, trying to find the best solution for the most people, or lessening your anxiety? If you can keep the creativity of the IM on task, you will lessen the potential of side issues from your past coming up into your argument.

LISTENING DOESN'T SEEM IMPORTANT

Due to the fact that IMs rely more on their own internal reality when they process life, they believe that listening to or really hearing other people is less important.

They are not trying to consciously be rude to, interrupt, or silence you. They really believe they know what you are going to say through your posture, tone, and history of previous conversations. Remember that speed has value, so they think it's good that they know what you're going to say—they can move more quickly to the next point or decision.

Because they are processing internally, they are not as focused on what you are saying as much as what they will say back to get you further along in the process. You see, for IMs you are not in a conversation so much as in a process of negotiating or deciding. IMs do not purposelessly refrain from sharing; they just want words and ideas to have a purpose.

This strength can also be a huge weakness. It's great to be able to move things forward, but not at the expense of a human heart. Regardless of the level of relevancy, articulation, speed, or emotional energy, hearts, especially those in a marriage, need to be heard. Ignoring feelings for the purpose of getting somewhere is always a mistake.

Jesus is not glorified when we don't hear our spouses' hearts. He doesn't value decisions or speed over people. People are what He came and died for.

The Maker of all we see and enjoy chooses to listen even when our best conversation is baby talk or gibberish to Him. This is critical for the IM to understand.

Winning an argument or making a decision without hearing one's spouse is wrong in the eyes of our Father God. How we listen and respond to our spouses is very important to Him.

As an IM, I've learned that I should lovingly listen to Lisa even if I don't agree. It is a bigger priority than being right. As an IM, you have to realize that you *can't* read minds or guess other people's thoughts, and you shouldn't form conclusions before the other person is finished speaking.

Good listening is an earmark of a mature IM. When IMs realize that all people have value at all times, and those people's hearts always have a higher value than ideas, the IMs have come a very long way. Listening is a skill, one you have to practice to perfect. If you believe you are an IM, try this with your spouse for sixty days: listen to his or her entire sentence before even starting a response. You will be amazed at how wise he or she really is! You'll find you can benefit by expanding from only your ideas to both of your ideas.

PERSISTENT

This gift is hardwired into IMs. They have almost endless persistence. When they lock onto a goal (usually their own, not someone else's), they are amazing to watch. Late nights, endless phone calls, hard work: it's all part of the process of achieving their goal.

This is a great gift when the Lord can utilize it, that is, if an IM has matured enough to allow God to share his ideas and know that God's ideas are better than his or her own. If the Lord tells IMs to do something, they will push through amazing obstacles to get where He told them to go. If they have an idea to achieve something, even if it will take years, they will get there—they will persist to the end. That is the blessing of this trait.

If you, however, are in the way of an IM's goal, be ready to be interacted with regularly and tirelessly. You will have to respond to endless arguments as to why you should go along with this idea.

IMs really believe that with persistence and effort, anything can be accomplished. Sadly, when IMs meet a situation in which persistence will not guarantee results, they can experience real sadness and self-doubt about their resources, intellect, or abilities. As a counselor, I have seen this in many marriages. One person won't love and won't try, and the IM spouse tirelessly tries to get the other's love—to no avail.

If your spouse is an IM, sometimes he or she will use this characteristic for you, and sometimes he or she will use it against you. You will have to help your spouse redirect his or her persistence toward a solution or deflect it to a spiritual authority. Sometimes an authority in that area of life can also move the train of this persistence away from you and in a more constructive direction.

You may love that your spouse doesn't quit when doing something you both agree on, but you can feel wounded when you feel you are in the way, even if you're right. You can face relentless pressure. If you feel you're right, stay your ground and call in help to mentor both of you through this particular decision or process.

*   *   *

In conclusion, let's look again at the traits of IMs. Internally motivated people:

- Think outside the box.
- Practice relative thinking.
- Overestimate their own ideas.
- Value speedy decisions.
- Rarely think about consequences.
- Accept conflict as part of life.
- Don't value responding or listening to others.
- Have tremendous persistence.

If you are married to an IM, hopefully you were able to see more of the gift this person can be to you. I hope you could see some of his or her behavior and processes through a more complete lens. The IM spouse is and always will be different from you.

Whether we are internally or externally motivated, as Christians we are in a lifelong process of becoming Christlike. Regardless of our motivation, we are equals in the sight of God. We are gifts to each other. In my opinion, gifts need to be celebrated. Celebrate your spouse regularly for who he/she is, and how God has made him/her to be a blessing to you and to those around you.

Before we cover more support principles for your marriage, I want you to take a moment to breathe. If you go too fast through the support principles, you might undervalue one that could have the potential to really help your marriage become successful.

Take some time right now to get out a piece of paper and answer the following questions:

- What did I learn about the externally motivated person?
- How can I apply what I learned to my marriage?
- What did I learn about the internally motivated person?
- How can I apply what I learned to my marriage?

You deserve the best marriage possible, and if you use these support principles, you will see encouraging results. I hope by now you have begun incorporating the three exercises to practice the Ten-Minute Marriage Principle so that you are already making that core relationship muscle group strengthen.

As you read these chapters on internal and external motivation, you have received a key to help you in your marriage. You can better understand how your spouse is made and how to better communicate. Improved understanding and communication will bolster your use of the exercises as well as help you resolve conflict more effectively. You and your spouse will grow closer and become more of a team.

If you are up for more, keep turning the pages!

7

THE ONE-MINUTE TURNAROUND

Over years of being married, either you or your spouse can suffer what I call a *spouse attack*. I don't mean those times when your spouse is yelling at you, although that might happen as well. Rather what I mean by a spouse attack is having a moment when, all of a sudden, out of the blue, a flood of negative thoughts hit you about the person you married.

Spouse attacks are almost like panic attacks: they're that unexpected and almost that frightening. You're suddenly focused on all of the bad things your husband or wife has or hasn't done over all the years of your relationship. Yes, spouse attacks are normal; they happen to many of us now and again. These attacks can be more severe during periods of financial, sexual, parental, or personal stress. They can happen the day after a big emotional confrontation. They can also move in when you realize your spouse isn't going to change the way you want him or her to, and you begin to feel hopeless about it.

Spouse attacks are very real. How you handle these

attacks can influence you and your marriage for days, weeks, or even longer. Sometimes you may not be the one having the attack—it may be that your spouse is suddenly acting and treating you differently.

Spouse attacks can overpower the way we see and treat our loved ones. We may be more suspicious, negative, angry, sarcastic, or unaffectionate toward our spouses. Our behavior can become sour and mean-spirited. We begin to believe that any negative aspects about our spouses are permanent.

When we experience spouse attacks, it's as if we have taken mental photographs of our husbands and wives. In these photos, however, are only a few of our spouses' traits that don't work well for us personally. We stare at these negative portrayals of our spouses to the exclusion of all the other amazing qualities they have.

Understanding a spouse attack can definitely help you as you practice your Ten-Minute Marriage Principle. If you know the storm you're in is temporary, you will navigate through the storm better. The same is true of spouse attacks. If you realize that you're focusing on your spouse's negative traits and ignoring his/her positive traits altogether, you know this bad feeling toward your spouse is temporary. You will stay steady with your exercises and applications of the support principles you have learned, and you will come out of the storm with little wear and tear on your marriage.

I will warn you, though, that spouse attacks have caused some relational casualties. This occurs when a person doesn't realize he's having a spouse attack and he thinks his spouse is truly all bad. He stops doing the three daily exercises in the Ten-Minute Marriage Principle. He grows more distant. He voices his dissatisfaction with his spouse repeatedly and creates pain that will last for days or more.

If instead you can identify a spouse attack when you have one, you can cling to the good qualities of your relationship, continue investing in it via the Ten-Minute Marriage Principle, and see your marriage grow.

Let me walk you through the common spouse attacks that a husband and wife might hear in their heads. I've compiled this example based on many years of listening to people who were right in the middle of spouse attacks. Before you read this, remember that your spouse also thinks very positive thoughts about you!

JACK AND BECKY

Let us observe spouse attacks on Jack and Becky. Jack and Becky have been married twenty-three years. They work together and have four children. Jack's spouse attack strikes early in the day. He rises before Becky because she takes the children to school, then comes in to their insurance office. Jack has just taken a shower and is preparing to get dressed when it happens.

Jack begins to think about his sleeping wife. He can't remember the last time she rolled over and gave him a kiss good morning. Then he can't think of the last time she initiated sex, wore a negligee, cooked a real meal for him, spent a weekend just with him, touched his back, rubbed his feet, or made his needs more important than those of any of their children or the dog.

He is just a grunt who's around to move this, pick up that, and make sure a child gets from Point A to Point B. Becky doesn't appreciate him for all the work he does to pay the huge bills every week. He can't remember the last time she was really interested in his dreams or even initiated a conversation that didn't have a task attached to it. He feels as if other women would appreciate him or at least talk to him. After all, he is a good provider and nice guy, even if he does have less hair than he used to.

You might be thinking, *Wow!* But this is a very common male spouse attack. By the time he drives to work, Jack already feels trapped by his marriage. He feels hopeless, alone, frustrated, and more importantly, unwanted by and insignificant to his wife.

Becky wakes up an hour later. She has to rouse what they call the "munchkins." She showers quickly, gets dressed, puts out the cereal, bread, and butter, then dries her hair. She drives her Chevrolet Suburban out of the driveway and it begins: listening to the constant bickering and fussing among the children. *This is twenty minutes of daily misery*, she thinks. She gets to one school, drops two children off, then on her way to the second school a child cries out, "Oh no, I don't have my math paper! Mr. Jones will give me a C if I don't have it by fourth period!" Becky, overwhelmed, tells the crying child she will retrieve the paper for her.

Then it hits: the spouse attack. Becky is just driving along with the bag of dry cleaning, taking the dog to get groomed, then heading to the office to get some work done there as well. But before she goes to the office, she's got to pick up and deliver her daughter's math paper. The attack starts: *Where is Jack, and why can't he ever help me? Why do I get stuck with all the kids' stuff? He is so selfish. All he does is work, come home, eat, and watch television. He's not a spiritual leader; he doesn't care about my world, my feelings; when was the last time he just held me and did not ask for sex?*

I hate how self-centered and pigheaded he is. He thinks that just because he is a man, he can do whatever he wants. I give and give, and he wants to know if he can play golf with his buddies on Saturday. He doesn't even know that two of the children have a soccer game that morning, and friends are supposed to drop by that night. What is he thinking?

You can see how ugly these spouse attacks can get. These attacks affect more than your thoughts—they get your emotions all stirred as well. By the time Becky finally shows up at the office, Jack gives her a look that says, *It's nice of the princess to come to work.* He even says, "Good morning, princess." Inside she seethes, *You mean Cinderella.*

If this sounds familiar, you want to know next how to handle these awful periods. First, let's look at some of the characteristics of a spouse attack. When you see these characteristics in yourself, you know you are right in the middle of the storm. Then you can take action to stop it.

CHARACTERISTICS OF A SPOUSE ATTACK

SELF-PITY

That sneaky feeling that nobody appreciates you is usually a major theme of a spouse attack. You are to be pitied because your spouse does not understand, appreciate, or validate you.

You are always the one who gives more love, service, money, or effort or deals with the issues that really matter in life. You are, after all, the real hero in the family and marriage.

Self-pity is tricky. It is a feeling—and such feelings don't have to be based on fact for you to feel them powerfully. If you think feelings are always true, you are in real trouble in a spouse attack. Whenever you start to feel self-pity, it is best to stop and challenge what you are thinking and feeling.

It really takes two heroes to do marriage well. It also takes two heroes to raise a family. In all honesty, in most cases, if our spouses didn't do their parts, we would really be in a jam.

I know that Lisa, my wife, is amazing. She is amazing not only in all she does at the home and office, but in the way she thinks. There have been countless times where just her perspective on a situation, relationship, or the children changed everything. My wife is a real gift and self-pity tends to get me to focus on me too much. Sometimes it is just laughable!

GLOBALIZING THE NEGATIVE

Every human being who walks Planet Earth has short-comings. All of us have areas of weaknesses that irritate our spouses. All of us can be forgetful, stubborn, selfish, and irrational. In theory we might believe this, but when we marry, we expect to be different—and we expect our spouses to be different, too—you know, caring.

Honestly, most of us don't deserve the spouses we have. Think about it: doesn't your spouse have great moments of coming through for you, showing you love, picking up the kids, and giving you time for yourself? When you get into a spouse attack, you quickly forget just how wonderful your spouse really is. You may think he or she "always" or "never" does something. If he is selfish, he is always, totally selfish. If she is unapprecia-tive, she is always completely unappreciative.

When you're having a spouse attack, you globalize the problem—make it more frequent and far-reaching than it is. You globalize the bad and annihilate the good of your spouse. Your former hero or heroine is now the enemy of your soul.

Even writing this stuff, I can see how silly it seems. But I know exactly how a spouse attack feels (more on that later in the chapter).

If you let the feelings and thoughts go on too long, you may come to actually believe that what you're feel-ing and globalizing is real. You're locked into a "real-ity" you just manufactured. Such "realities" need to be nipped in the bud.

You see, when you globalize your spouse's negative characteristics, you can become blind to who he or she really is. It's as if your spouse goes into the proverbial telephone booth and instead of coming out with a superhero suit on, he or she comes out like Darth Vader, ready to destroy anything good in your life. Now your spouse is your nemesis!

When you begin to globalize your situation, you get too emotional to see clearly or react well to others. You become critical, which makes life with you just a little less fun.

ETERNALIZING THE BAD

In a spouse attack, on top of the spouse's being all bad, you *eternalize* his or her faults. You unofficially declare that this one negative photograph you have of your spouse is permanent instead of seeing your spouse in a series of pictures like a motion picture. In a motion picture, in each scene the hero does something different: sometimes a good thing, sometimes another good thing, and then a blooper. The blooper is just one picture! When you are in a spouse attack, the blooper scene is eternal. It's as if you pause your DVD on the villain— your spouse—and freeze the photo there.

We are all capable of bad attitudes, beliefs, and behaviors at any time. That is what makes us human. We are all flawed but loved.

As we get better at handling spouse attacks, we will be able to focus on the lovely parts of our spouses as well.

You know that you're actually handling the spouse attack better when you can get your finger off the pause button when your spouse has made a mistake. Instead you can push Rewind and revisit the positive memories about your spouse from earlier scenes in this movie you call your marriage. You can also push Fast-Forward and see the potentially positive experiences you will have as you walk through the future together. When this happens, you then will know that you have learned how to victoriously handle a spouse attack.

DOOMED

Once you wallow in self-pity, globalize the problem, and eternalize the negative, you feel doomed. You naturally conclude that you are the hopeless victim of this once-decent person. Feeling doomed for me is always a red flag. It always makes me stop to question whether what I feel is real or just what I feel. Outside of having a terrorist hold a loaded gun held next to my head, I can feel doomed, but I'm not.

Like other feelings, feelings of doom will pass. Take that feeling for what it is: a red flag that you are unsuccessfully dealing with your spouse attack. In fact, any moment now, this globalized, eternalized, negative person will probably come to say or do something that makes you realize why you loved him or her to begin with!

So many people I see in counseling succumb to feeling doomed. They get sucked into this dark room on how bad everything is in their lives. They internally see only large photographs of their spouses' shortcomings or failures. They feel stuck in hopelessly bad marriages.

This is a great time to pray—really pray and thank God for His wisdom to bless you with such a spouse.

Take the time to tell God what blesses you about your spouse. It works for me every time.

"I HAVE NO RESPONSIBILITY"

When you're in a spouse attack, you get into black-and-white or "all or nothing" thinking. The spouse is then 100 percent of the issue, and you are 0 percent of the problem. There is no way the spouse's bad behavior is even partially your fault.

Jack and Becky's spouse attacks contained some facts. It was true Jack didn't ask how to get involved with Becky's day the night before. His assuming that she would handle most of the family details is a fact. Becky's not kissing Jack first thing in the morning for over three years is also a fact.

If you engage in black-and-white thinking, you'll see both of these facts on the black side and entitle the other spouse to resentment. Could it be that Jack feels abandoned emotionally, so he abandons Becky in return? Could it be that Becky feels Jack's abandonment of her and the children's responsibilities, so she abandons Jack in a way that hurts him?

See, when you are not in a spouse attack you can see some of the cause and effect. You can also usually see that there may be reasons behind the two behaviors that can be worked out. Jack and Becky could easily negotiate a steamy kiss in the morning in exchange for his picking up the children from school.

When you are using black-and-white or "all or nothing" thinking, be careful: you are probably in the midst of a spouse attack.

WINNING THE BATTLE:
THE ONE-MINUTE TURNAROUND

You can use several tools during a spouse attack.

POSITIVE STATEMENTS

I remember distinctly a spouse attack I had one day. It occurred over fifteen years ago when Lisa and I lived in Texas. I was driving home from work. I was only a few miles from home when, all of a sudden, every negative thought and feeling possible about my precious Lisa started hitting me. I remember thinking, *What is going on?*

I went from looking forward to going home to being angry at my wife. But I was a veteran of spouse attacks and knew how to skew the skirmish: I slowed down and said out loud, "Stop!" Then I started to say out loud the wonderful things I knew about my wife:

- "Lisa is a godly woman."
- "Lisa is a great lover."
- "Lisa is a great friend."
- "Lisa is absolutely gorgeous."
- "Lisa will always be a faithful woman."

What happened next was great. The spouse attack ceased! I was now looking forward to seeing my bride again; actually I was *really* looking forward to seeing her! It's as if I had been in a fight, and I won!

You are going to have spouse attacks. What you do

with them is critical. Instead of going with the thoughts and feelings, mount a counterattack. You need to be prepared to do this. Take out a sheet of paper. Write out five things you love, like, or value about your spouse.

Now say these things out loud to yourself somewhere. Say them with emotion because they are true! Memorize them so they'll be handy when you need them.

After I memorized those wonderful aspects of Lisa, I found that I had fewer spouse attacks, and I won the attacks that came. You can be successful, too.

Go ahead, time yourself. It will take you less than one minute to have success and win over a spouse attack. That's why I call it the One-Minute Turnaround, because in one minute you can go from the funk of a spouse attack to clarity on why you love this person!

PICTURES OF HAPPY TIMES

For those of you who think more visually—in pictures—I suggest that you not only memorize your five positive statements but collect five positive photographs of your spouse—either mental photos or photos on paper. Those of you who are tech-savvy can put some photos in your cell phones to help you remember the good times. (You can also use your phone to take pictures of good times when they happen.) If you get blindsided by a spouse attack, pull out the pictures of your spouse—whether they are mental images, paper photos, or cell-phone pictures—at these more positive times and remember that there will be more to come.

CALL A FRIEND

Talk to someone about the spouse attack. I don't mean seeing a counselor or pastor—although you may need to do this if spouse attacks become frequent and actually disrupt your relationship. I mean just calling a friend. Be certain, before you make the call, that your objective is to ask someone to pray for you—not to complain about your spouse. Don't call to expose your spouse's weaknesses to another person.

Rather call and say something like this: "I am having all kinds of negative thoughts [or feelings] about my spouse. I know I am not thinking clearly and my feelings are a mess. I need some help. Can you just pray that I can get out of this fog and be grateful for my spouse? Would you pray for me right now that God would help me get my head and heart in the right place?" Hearing your friend's prayer could be the catalyst for reigniting love for your spouse!

When you start getting a full-blown spouse attack, you now have three weapons. Decide within yourself that if a spouse attack occurs, you are going to pop that attack as you would a balloon: Pop! And it's over.

Use your statements and pictures immediately. By the time you get to the fifth picture, you will be able to see and think of your spouse more clearly and fondly. Or make the call before the thoughts change your mood. While you're using your Ten-Minute Marriage Principle Exercises, you're going to have many good days. But on the bad ones, if you feel a spouse attack coming, put these support principles to work. Attack back and win for your marriage. You'll learn to laugh at the storm as you speak to it and see it calm right before your eyes. Again, these methods can help you jump out of a spouse attack in *less than one minute*.

You can have a One-Minute Turnaround anytime you like. You *don't* have to stay in or suffer through a spouse attack. You can get regrounded and then work to actually solve the issues in your marriage. You deserve to feel good about your spouse as much as possible. So practice your One-Minute Turnarounds and utilize this tool in practicing the Ten-Minute Marriage Principle.

The Ten-Minute Marriage Principle is all about giving you positive tools to smooth out bumps that occur in a marriage. As these bumps get smoothed out, the better you both feel. It is possible you and your loved one will have a spouse attack on the same day. You'll know you are fighting it successfully when you both still have a great day!

8

THE TEN-MINUTE ARGUMENT

Tim and Darla were a precious seminary couple. Tim was from North Carolina and Darla from Alabama. Tim and Darla had just celebrated their third year of marriage. Tim had one more year of school left before he completed his master's in divinity. He had wanted to be a pastor his whole life. When other kids in his neighborhood wanted to play house or war, Tim wanted to play church and, yes, he was always the preacher.

Darla's parents were not Christians until she was in high school, when her dad lost his company to bankruptcy. Darla and Tim met in Bible college. They dated and stayed pure and accountable to their mentors at school. They married in their last year of college and lived on campus.

Tim and Darla looked like a young couple with so much promise. Tim could preach well, and Darla could touch your heart with a gospel song as few others her age could do. But according to Tim and Darla, they had a "huge problem." No, it wasn't money, sex, friends, or the church they faithfully attended. It took them a while to explain their problem between their apologies: "I'm embarrassed." "It's awful, and we both still want to be in the ministry." Finally Tim leaned toward me, took a breath, and blurted out: "We fight!"

I really felt this was anticlimactic. I was expecting some deep, dark secret in one of their souls, an affair or stealing money.

"You fight," I repeated. I didn't know what to say because I was so thrown off by Tim's anxiety about his revelation.

Tim went on to explain that he knows everybody disagrees from time to time, but that he and Darla really fight. He said he never saw his parents fight the way he and Darla did. He was very concerned that his marriage wouldn't make it and he'd never fulfill his call to ministry.

They told me the fights started about anything. The couple rapid-fired accusations and assumptions at each other. They eventually stooped to name-calling and occasionally even breaking things in their apartment. At the end, Tim usually walked out, but by then they were both wounded. To top it off, they were both so ashamed of the way they acted that they could barely talk about the issues that started the fight in fear of reigniting the bomb.

MEET JIM AND ALICE

Meet another couple. Jim and Alice are in their late fifties. Both Jim and Alice have suffered physical problems in the last few years—which they are quick to share with you early in the conversation. Jim is close to retiring from the engineering company he helped start many years ago. Alice has only months to go before she re-tires, having been a schoolteacher in the local elemen-tary school most of her career.

Jim and Alice have had a bumpy relationship most of their lives. They admit that raising their four children was the focus of their life for most of their marriage. They have regrets about neglecting their relationship, but they seem comfortable in the current disrepair—except for one issue.

"It's fighting," Jim scruffily stated. "We don't fight." As we continued, I could see Jim was accurate. Jim and Alice didn't fight or argue at all. They didn't talk about problems.

Their pattern for dealing with conflict was, if it got heated, Jim walked off and would not talk about it or anything else with Alice for days—sometimes even weeks. Alice usually ended up handling it, whatever "it" was. She had grown resentful because she felt alone and overwhelmed by some of the decisions she had to make. She always knew the silence was coming, so after a few days of pleading to talk, she just comforted herself with hot tea and cookies until Jim decided to talk again.

Facing retirement, Jim and Alice didn't want to live like this. Alice had threatened to move out and live at their vacation cabin for good if Jim didn't change.

THE REAL PROBLEM

The thing is, Tim and Darla and Jim and Alice have exactly the same problem. I know you're thinking, *Are you crazy? One couple screams and the other won't talk. How can that be the same problem?* Let me explain.

Tim and Darla don't know how to handle conflict. Tim saw little conflict growing up, and Darla is repeating behaviors she saw in her non-Christian childhood. Jim and Alice also don't know how to handle conflict either, so they don't talk. Both couples are poor at managing conflict. Both couples need a set of tools to learn how to fight.

Some great news about fighting: you can get it over with—no matter what the issue—in ten minutes. I'll show you how, just as I showed Tim, Darla, Jim, and Alice.

Imagine how Tim and Darla feel now that they can argue in less than ten minutes and actually get a conclusion. They have saved hours and hours of time—not to mention hurt feelings and frustration. Tim is now confident that ministry is a sure thing, and Darla is singing free of any guilt for the way she treats Tim.

Alice never did move to that cabin. Jim and Alice spent the summer together on the lake fishing and having children and friends over for their famous fish fries. Jim feels better as a man and as a husband to his bride. They both are less focused on what's wrong with their health.

What happened to these couples isn't a miracle, although it feels that way to them. What happened is both couples learned how to have the Ten-Minute Argument and actually get to a solution they could both live with.

You see, conflict is a part of every relationship. You will have conflict in your parent/child relationship regardless which role you are in. Conflict with friends, coworkers, employers, employees—it's just a natural part of life. And when handled well, conflict is actually a healthy part of life.

Conflict usually musters up several ideas to choose from. Conflict gives us a variety of perspectives and makes us think through matters. Conflict has helped me make better choices throughout my life and career.

Some of us have a skewed view of conflict. Some believe that winning is the only issue, no matter what the cost; forget rules and respect. Those who hold this view yell, shame, review past mistakes, call names, and basically act like children during a conflict.

The other extreme is avoiding conflict at all costs. Here silence, withholding love, affection, sex, and money are the tools a person uses. Unfortunately, this approach to conflict may sound nice, but nothing gets resolved and mountains of resentment can build up over time.

Again, conflict is normal and healthy and you should expect it in a healthy marriage—yes, even for Christians. You see, I don't have all truth and knowledge, and neither does my wife. In many instances, through conflict Lisa and I discover better ideas or options. If we can't, then we can always consult our team (see chapter 11).

Even as you practice the Ten-Minute Marriage Principle, you will still experience some conflict. I want to give you another support principle so that you can move through conflict and actually toward possible solutions. You see, conflict that doesn't actually get to a solution is just a warm-up for more conflict in the future.

If you actually agree on some solutions during a conflict, you will have fewer conflicts in the future. A couple that can successfully solve conflicts one by one can look forward to smoother sailing than their prickly counterparts. They will actually experience less and less conflict over the decades. Imagine all the time you can save and use to just enjoy each other!

In the following pages I will outline ten steps to have a Ten-Minute Argument. Read carefully and practice this process. You'll want to add this helpful support principle to your Ten-Minute Marriage Principle lifestyle. If you can work *proactively* to make your marriage better in just ten minutes a day, you can also work *reactively* to make your marriage better by resolving conflicts in just ten minutes a day!

TEN STEPS TO QUICKER FIGHTS

1. STATE ONE PROBLEM

I wish this were more profound. But it's simple. When couples start fighting, even in my office, they move from subject to subject. Some of this jumping around might just be human nature. Some we might attribute to poor role models, a lack of respect for others, or even just a desire to see if one's spouse goes for the bait. Regardless of the reason for jumping around, you have to state only one problem if you are going to have a Ten-Minute Argument.

Now, if you like arguing and it's your exercise for the evening, continue doing all the verbal gymnastics you wish. But you risk hurting feelings and having little ears hear Mom and Dad's fight. If you'd rather learn how to have a Ten-Minute Argument, you will need two tablets or pieces of paper. At the top of each piece of paper, clearly write what the problem is: "Our problem is _____ _____." My experience has shown that if a couple refuse to agree what the problem is, rarely will they have a Ten-Minute Argument.

As a matter of fact, clearly stating the problem keeps one or both partners from using unkind approaches to conflict. Not all couples fight to solve a problem. Some fight to establish who's the boss, who is in control, who has more anger or hate, who can think the fastest and manipulate the other person, or sometimes—believe it or not—just so they can kiss and make up.

As Paul said in 1 Corinthians 12:31: "Now I will show you the most excellent way." The best way for Christian couples to resolve conflict—the way that leads to peace, respect, and solutions—is to state one problem.

A fun way to interrupt an argument is to continue asking your spouse, "What exactly are we trying to resolve here?" If he or she is a "jumper," this can help him or her stay focused.

For now, just stick to paper and pen until the Ten-Minute Argument becomes second nature to you.

2. IDENTIFY FEELINGS

This is where most couples blow it big-time. Most of us have not had any training in identifying or communicating our feelings. This is where the Feelings exercise in chapter 2 can help you not only become more connected to your spouse, but learn how to stop fights as well. I can't recommend this exercise highly enough as one to do daily.

If either spouse cannot identify a wide range of feelings, your fights will last much longer than ten minutes. If a spouse is emotionally stuck and unskilled at communicating, it can take hours to get to what he or she feels about an issue, his or her spouse, and/or him- or herself.

When we humans get in a conflict, rarely is it without emotion. The conflict might appear to be small but the emotions attached may be huge. For the Ten-Minute Argument to work, both spouses need to list three to five feelings about the problem stated in step 1. On your sheets of paper, make lists like these:

State the Problem

His Feelings	Her Feelings
1. _____	1. _____
2. _____	2. _____
3. _____	3. _____
4. _____	4. _____
5. _____	5. _____

It's very important that *both* spouses list their feelings. If one doesn't, those feelings will usually show up in less-direct and unhealthy ways.

After you write down your feelings, don't talk about them yet. Take a second look at the feelings you listed and make sure that they are related to the problem at hand—not to some other issue. This is an important step. You see, sometimes our feelings about an issue go back to an earlier time in our relationships or even all the way back to our childhoods.

Blake and Eve experienced this in their marriage again and again when they were in conflict. When Blake was a boy, his mom would yell at him and he wasn't allowed to respond in any way. He felt controlled, unheard, and manipulated in almost every conflict with his wife, Eve. His feelings were not really about Eve, though. His feelings stemmed from the way his mother conditioned him to believe that conflicts were not about solutions or ideas but control.

So when you look at the feelings you wrote down, be careful that these feelings are related to the current conflict and not another source. Try to avoid using feelings to attack your spouse. Remember that in a Ten-Minute Argument your spouse is your ally toward a solution, not the enemy in the battle over who is right and who is wrong.

3. CREATE SOLUTIONS

This may be a novel idea for some couples: create multiple solutions. Most problems or issues can be solved in several different ways. When you fight believing you are all right and your spouse is all wrong, rarely are you fighting about the issue. Rather you're battling over the heavyweight title of Mr. or Mrs. Right.

The right-and-wrong paradigm limits creativity. The spouses are so busy trying to prove who's right that they fail even to look for a solution. I always tell my clients there are at least three ways to solve most problems. Now, you might not like some of the options, but they are still options.

When you choose to create options, you utilize the creative strengths of both people to solve the problem. Harnessing creativity for solving the problem is so much better than using your creativity to out-shout or out-manipulate each other.

Let's look at how this actually works. Ed and Renee argue about who should clean up after dinner. After writing their feelings about this, they write out their solutions on their pieces of paper:

Ed's Solutions	Renee's Solutions
Renee should do it.	Ed should do it.
I could do it.	I could do it.
Kids could do it.	Rotate kids to do it by the week, each gets one week.
	Use paper and plastic plates and each person is responsible to throw theirs away.
	Each person puts their plates and cups away.

Rotate: each day one
person in family does it all.

Hire a maid to do it.

My example is in no way a gender slam on male creativity (remember, I am one). It just so happens that Renee put more thought into this particular problem, as you can see.

4. COMMUNICATE

After all this writing, it's time to talk. Start with the agreed-upon one problem. Then let each person share his or her feelings about the problem. When someone is sharing his or her feelings, you need to listen carefully. Look that person in the eye and really try to hear with your heart. Heart-to-heart communication is the best, not head-to-head. Also, as you're listening, give *absolutely no feedback*. You are listening, not judging or assessing.

This is a critical point to remember. Saying nothing might require strong discipline on your part, but stick with it. If you comment, your spouse will defend him- or herself and you will be off to the races. Feelings are feelings, not facts. In my more than eighteen years of counseling, I have rarely heard someone tell another person what he or she should feel and then find a solution to a conflict. Judging each other's emotional responses could easily sidetrack you, so please don't succumb to the temptation to give feedback at this juncture.

Then move on to the solutions. In our example with Ed and Renee, both of them would share their lists of creative solutions. Again, when sharing solutions, there is no feedback. If you start giving feedback, you can short-circuit the process and get into an argument. In the Ten-Minute Argument, you don't need to get into judgments and yelling at each other. Simply go to the next step of the process.

5. COMBINE YOUR LISTS

When you have two brilliant people in the same marriage, you will probably come up with the same ideas. The next step is to each take the other's ideas and add them to your tablet.

In the case of Ed and Renee, they would each create a combined list:

- Ed could do it.
- Renee could do it.
- Rotate kids to do it by the week, each gets one week.
- Use paper and plastic plates and each person is responsible to throw theirs away.
- Each person puts their plates and cups away.
- Rotate: each day one person in the family does it all.
- Hire a maid to do it.

Write your combined lists on your separate tablets so you can take the next step in the Ten-Minute Argument.

6. VOTE

That's right: you get to vote on your options! I know this takes all the anger, manipulation, and making up later out of the equation, but imagine the time and energy you can save!

The voting process is simple. Each of you gives a weighted response to each idea. Vote on each idea with a number from one to ten. A one vote means you *really do not like* this particular idea. A ten vote means you *really like* this idea. Each item gets a number.

I will warn you: if you vote all ones or all tens, you basically are giving your spouse the ability to make the decisions by the way he or she votes. An idea you largely disagree on rarely wins. If one spouse votes one and the other votes ten, that gives the option a score of eleven. Somewhere else one will vote a six or seven, the spouse will do the same, and that idea will get a greater number of points than the ten and one.

7. COMBINE VOTES

Then take your votes and place them on one piece of paper. Here are Ed and Renee's responses.

Ed's Vote		Renee's Vote
4	Ed could do it.	7
8	Renee could do it.	3
7	Rotate kids to do it by the week, each gets one week.	7

Ed's Vote		Renee's Vote
4	Use paper and plastic plates and each person is responsible to throw theirs away.	6
6	Each person puts their plates and cups away.	7
8	Rotate: each day one person in the family does it all.	9
1	Hire a maid to do it.	2

8. GO WITH THE HIGHEST VOTE

As you can see, Ed and Renee, like every couple, varied in their responses. The highest vote, however, was not for just one of them do the work; rather the highest vote was for rotations—each person in the family having the task of cleaning up after dinner.

Ed and Renee didn't have to raise their voices, slam doors, or dislike each other for hours to get to this conclusion. Problems big or small *can* be solved in ten minutes. The toughest part is just going with the highest vote. Sometimes we are so emotionally invested in a certain outcome that we want to huff and puff to try to get our way. If you can restrain yourself, you can have a solution in ten minutes or less.

It is possible in your voting to come to a tie. This can be fun, especially if you are feeling as if your idea is the better one and should again win. There is a great way to solve a tie without further voting or gnashing of teeth.

Simply pull a coin from your pocket, purse, or junk drawer. One of you calls "heads" and the other calls "tails." That's right, you're flipping a coin. The winner wins and that is that. One of you gets to smile and one acts mature and congratulates the other and moves on.

9. RECORD YOUR DECISION

When a couple comes to a solution for handling a difficult situation, it's helpful to have a clear way to remember their agreement. You want a way to record your agreed-upon method so you can both easily be reminded exactly what it was.

Couples can create a record of this event in several ways. This could be done on a cassette or a CD labeled Decisions; entries should be titled and dated. Couples can keep a document on computer that keeps a record of their decisions. (A caution here, though: in a weak moment, someone could delete or revise the entire document. This will only create more conflict!)

My personal favorite application of this idea is to keep a handwritten record in a notebook. Some couples purchase a nice leather-bound notebook, and others just go to Office Depot or Wal-Mart and get the inexpensive notebooks that students purchase.

Some couples go as far as to name this notebook. This can actually be helpful to cement the purpose of this book in the life of your marriage. Here are some names couples have used:

The Final Word

Declaration of Decisions

The Captain's Log (*Star Trek* fans)

The _____ Book (Last name in blank)

To Be Remembered

In this log or record you must list the date, the conflict, and the decision. Let me give you an example. Jason and Jennifer were your typical happy-go-lucky couple. They married in college, both have corporate jobs, and they have two teenage children and a show dog named Tucker. Life is peaceful at Jason and Jennifer's house except when they disagree. Here are some samples from their log:

Date: 1/15/07
Issue: Arranging pickup for the boys at school and basketball practice.

Decision: Jennifer is responsible for this on Monday, Tuesday, and Wednesday. Jason is responsible for this on Thursday, Friday, and Saturday. We can switch days if we give each other twenty-four hours' notice. This decision stays in place until the end of the basketball season.

Date: 2/9/07
Issue: Mark, our accountant, recommended we put 40 percent of our portfolio into the ABC investment, which had a higher risk and higher potential yield.

Decision: We decided not to change our portfolio. Jason will communicate this to Mark by phone and by fax.

Date: 3/21/07
Issue: Brian's birthday party

Decision: We will have a family party and spend no more than a total of three hundred dollars on the birthday party and gifts.

10. SIGN YOUR AGREEMENT

Be sure to sign off on each entry in your log. Even if the entry addresses only one person's behavior, you both need to sign the entry.

This is valuable for future discussions that come up as to whether you or our spouse really did agree to such and such.

I know if I sign something, I do so only after I really read and reflect on the proposal before me. I know I am committing myself explicitly to an agreed-upon action. And I remember my commitment better if it requires a John Hancock from me. This is true for many: signing off does somehow cement the agreement in your memory.

So if I make a decision with my spouse, write out the agreement, and sign off on it, I can fortify myself against having spousal amnesia. When the temptation comes to make a unilateral decision, I will be much more likely to revisit the temptation and honor my agreements.

There you have it: ten simple steps, ten short minutes, to a more peaceful marriage!

FAILURE TO FOLLOW THROUGH

There's just one problem when you've reached a conclusion to a fight: both of you then must abide by the decision. But as a counselor, I have seen many times that even after the Ten-Minute Argument, one partner changes his or her mind about the outcome, fails to follow through on his or her commitment to the decision, and the conflict re-escalates.

Does this sound familiar? You work through a multifaceted situation. You and your spouse agree, kiss good night, and go to sleep. Later the next day, you check in with each other and one of you has done the opposite of—or something completely different from—what you decided the night before. Why does a spouse do this? There are several reasons.

REASONS WHY SPOUSES FAIL TO FOLLOW THROUGH

First, you or your spouse could be suffering from temporary spousal amnesia. This happens to millions of couples. One spouse doesn't remember what the other spouse said earlier. It has disappeared from his or her mind. Some spouses actually forget momentarily that they are married at all and think unilateral decisions are their right.

All of us are capable of mental glitches. As I age, I find this happening more—most of us do. This isn't malicious; it's human.

Second, you or your spouse may truly believe your relationship is a monarchy. One of you believes that he or she has—and deserves to have—the final word. Even Christians sometimes get selfish in marriage.

Third, on a more serious note, one spouse could have Attention Deficit Hyperactive Disorder (ADHD). Yes, children aren't the only ones who suffer from this condition. If a spouse is *constantly* forgetting, seems always distracted, and fails repeatedly to get things done, seek professional help. These husbands and wives are truly not trying to be frustrating or forgetful; they just live moment by moment and, through no fault of their own, they simply can't focus.

Let's return to our couple, Jason and Jennifer. One of them decides to act against their decision again and again (I'll keep the culprit's name to myself). Regardless of why Jason or Jennifer would agree to something and then do differently, this lack of follow-through hurts their otherwise happy marriage for days to come. You can imagine all the energy that goes into developing a solution and then bam, nothing is actually resolved. The offended spouse may feel confusion, betrayal, and/or anger.

THE SOLUTION

So how do we help couples like Jason and Jennifer when this mistake occurs on a semiregular basis? If the problem isn't a disorder like ADHD, there is a simple solution. This idea reduces the occurrences of these situations and sets consequences for the person who has these lapses of memory or follow-through from time to time.

When you record your decision in your log, follow it with consequences for each spouse should he or she fail to follow through. Understand, though, that the *consequence* isn't a *punishment*. A punishment exists when one spouse plays the role of being the parent to the other spouse. He or she decides the punishment for the "child's" bad behavior.

In marriage, treating each other like adults is important. It is also important to act like adults. So if I break my word, I should have a consequence that I set up for *myself*.

If I break my word and the only pain I feel is the disappointment my spouse expresses, that might not be enough to make me change my behavior. If, however, my failure will cause *me* some pain, I might think about it before breaking my word. And when I suffer a consequence I set up for myself, I can't blame anyone for it. This way, as an adult you spank yourself for inappropriate behavior, and you feel the pain of your bad choices.

Let me give you some ideas of consequences that clients have set up if they break an agreement. Of course this is only a short list of examples, but you can get a general idea and apply your creativity to this process. Remember, you are looking *only* for ideas that apply to yourself.

- Taking a two-mile run
- Picking up trash for two to four hours
- Giving four hours' time to an organization you don't support

- Giving time/money to a person you don't really like
- Giving an item you like (shoes, golf clubs) away
- Doing extra chores around the house (clean garage, paint a room)
- Giving spouse an hour-and-a-half massage
- Giving spouse money to do as he or she wishes
- Giving up TV for two weeks

A word of caution on your consequence: choose one that doesn't take away time with your spouse or family as a punishment to them. For instance, if you choose to pick up trash for two hours, don't do it at Saturday midday. Instead, tackle your consequence from 6:00 AM to 8:00 AM so it is out of the way.

RECORD THE CONSEQUENCE

Now that you have the idea of consequences figured out, you can record this in your decision log. Let's go back to Jason and Jennifer's log for examples.

Date: 1/15/07

Issue: Arrange to pick up boys from school and basketball practice.

Decision: Jennifer is responsible for this on Monday, Tuesday, and Wednesday. Jason is responsible for this on Thursday, Friday, and Saturday. We can switch a day if we give each other twenty-four hours' notice. This decision stays in place until the end of basketball season.

Consequence: Jason's consequence for not picking up the boys on his days or without warning that something important came up is that he has to transport the boys all the next week on his own. Jennifer agrees to the same consequence.

Date: 3/21/07

Issue: Brian's birthday party

Decision: We will have a family party and spend no more than three hundred dollars on the birthday party and gifts.

Consequence: Jennifer agrees that if she spends over three hundred dollars, she will run two miles for two days. Jason will pick up trash two hours for two days.

Remember the step of signing off on your agreements *and* their consequences. When you begin utilizing this support principle to keep written records of your agreements and the consequences for breaking an agreement, you are contributing even more to the lifestyle of the Ten-Minute Marriage Principle. As you learn to resolve conflicts, you make the exercises even easier to do—and your relationship warmer and more inviting.

I enjoy liking Lisa. When conflict comes or decisions have to be made, I want the process to be as smooth as possible with the least amount of emotional damage to each other or our marriage. Our Ten-Minute Argument plan keeps our affection strong and lasting, even through conflict.

IN SUMMARY

Here is a review of the process. Try this with at least three problems and see what you think of the Ten-Minute Argument.

The Ten-Minute Argument Process

1. State the problem (using separate tablets).
2. Identify feelings (using separate tablets).
3. Create solutions (using separate tablets).
4. Communicate.
5. Create a mutual list.
6. Vote (on separate tablets).
7. Combine votes.
8. Go with the highest vote.
9. Record your decision.
10. Sign your decision.

Again, if necessary, set consequences for yourselves in case you don't follow through.

I wish you happy arguing! In living out the Ten-Minute Marriage Principle you can have Ten-Minute Arguments. Again, the Ten-Minute Argument is one of the several support principles available to help you have a smoother marriage. If you are doing your Ten-Minute Exercises and add the Ten-Minute Argument, you will be fighting less and enjoying each other more. Once you learn how to argue, you argue better and everyone wins! Arguing is part of marital life. But it doesn't need to be ugly, shaming, or in any way harmful. You both have great ideas and resources to solve problems. God has put you together so that you can be a team to solve most of the things that come your way.

If you can escape the trap of someone's being right and someone's being wrong, you can save your marriage immeasurable pain over the years. Try it. Ahead of you might just be the peaceful world of the Ten-Minute Argument.

9

MARITAL KRYPTONITE

In the age of the comic book comeback, superheroes surround us. We have the X-Men, Spiderman, and of course the leader of the pack, Superman. I love Superman. He can fly, he's strong, he has a real job, and he struggles with female relationships. Even though he has laser vision and can repel bullets and save the world, he also has a weakness.

His weakness is kryptonite, a stone from his planet of origin. Just being in the presence of kryptonite forces the mighty man of steel to his knees. It's not just Superman, though: most of our heroes and heroines have weak spots. I think this makes our heroes more relatable to us. Who doesn't love it when Superman's alter ego, Clark Kent, is fumbling through a conversation with Lois Lane?

As with our heroes, even those living the Ten-Minute Marriage Principle can have some sort of kryptonite that can weaken the marriage. Some of these weaknesses are created long before we marry.

In the movie *Ice Age,* a prehistoric squirrel provides

comic relief. He is constantly trying to obtain or keep his precious acorn. He tends to thump his acorn into the ground. His pounding the acorn creates these little cracks in the earth. The cracks travel quickly over great land masses and create some sort of natural disaster.

As people we also sometimes receive cracks early in life that, if not addressed, creating significant pain in our relationships. I want to cover four of these possible kryptonites that can create pain even while you're trying to live your Ten-Minute Marriage Principle.

You may not have any of these issues. As a counselor, I know, though, that many couples do, so I need to cover them for those couples' long-term success in marriage. Also, throughout the course of your marriage you will know several couples that may be limping along because of one of these major issues in one or both of their lives.

1. ABUSE

Chet and Maryann are a couple who were caught off guard by a crack in their marriage. Chet was in his late thirties, handsome, and successful in his corporate career. He grew up on a farm in Kansas. He remembered helping out on the farm before he even started first grade. His dad worked from five in the morning until seven or eight that night.

Chet's dad was constantly critical. Chet couldn't remember one kind word of approval from his father. Dad was also verbally abusive toward everyone, family or not. Dad wasn't afraid to hit his children or his wife.

Chet, however, had a sincere heart to please others, especially Dad, but to no avail. Eventually Chet went to college and started working in a big city two states away. He met Maryann at church and they fell in love.

Everything looked normal in this relationship, but the crack of physical and emotional abuse began to take its toll. The wounds from Chet's dad were not healed. He couldn't ever receive praise from Maryann, so he felt unappreciated. If he had feelings he wouldn't talk about them—he would just bury himself in his work. Chet's inability to receive love seemed to be getting worse.

Chet was a survivor of abuse. In his case he was emotionally neglected and physically abused by his father. Thus conflict wasn't Chet's strong suit. Maryann also had some abuses that she had never told Chet about. As a teenager growing up in the city, she was raped by an older man. She kept this secret inside and blamed herself. This crack grew over the years in her life, and she eventually showed symptoms of being a sexual abuse survivor.

People get abused in many ways. For some it's physical and emotional abuse or neglect. Many have suffered sexual abuse or rape as a child, adolescent, or adult. Abuse impacts every person differently. It catapults some to work through the wounds. Others build walls or habits to protect themselves. Some of these walls or habits are more destructive than others. Regardless of how one reacts, these reactions can seriously impact a marriage.

Having wounds from the past myself, I knew I had to work to make sure that Lisa was not going to have to deal with any cracks from my abuse. To heal from past abuse, you first have to acknowledge that the abuse really did occur. Second, you need to place responsibility on the person who actually committed the abuse. Third, some anger counseling is usually very helpful. Fourth, you need to move into forgiveness.

It's important to note that as people move through trauma, they will also go through various stages of grief. They'll have to own and release what happened to them and the consequences in their lives. Grief is a process that moves us through denial, anger, bargaining, and sadness toward acceptance.

As a counselor for as many years, I know abuse and neglect impact every soul differently. For some, just walking through the process I outlined can bring great relief. For others, getting professional counseling may be necessary to heal the wounds incurred in their particular journeys through life.

Regardless of the wounds you may have experienced as a child, adolescent, or adult, you *can* heal from them. You and your spouse are worthy of a healthy and happy marriage. I know, personally and professionally, that as someone actively heals, his or her marriage becomes easier and so much more fulfilling for both people.

Next we'll look at a common kind of abuse that can impact marriages and what to do about it.

ABANDONMENT

Abandonment is a form of emotional abuse. Meet another couple—Marty and Charise. Marty and Charise were in their late twenties. Marty was in the ministry and loved it. Charise was an elementary school teacher.

They were a delightful couple to everyone who knew them. They had two children, a boy and a girl.

Marty's "crack" began early in his life. You see, Marty's mom became pregnant with him her last year of high school. Marty's biological dad abandoned Mom and has, to this day, never seen Marty.

Marty's mom did the best she could by living with her parents so she could go to college. She didn't date for years, but when Marty was eight she married the man who became Marty's stepdad. Marty's stepdad was a traveling salesman who didn't take much interest in Marty. Thus both Marty's dad and his stepdad abandoned him. Three years after they were married, Marty's stepdad divorced his mother.

Marty thought he had dealt with this because of his faith. But he made comments about the time someday when (he believed) Charise would leave him. After the first couple of years of marriage, Marty closed down emotionally. He wouldn't receive the love Charise had for him and doubted her motives. He had outbursts of anger disproportionate to the situations. Marty's abandonment crack started to show up. He didn't want it to, but he seemed powerless to stop the crack from growing in his life and marriage.

Abandonment can go very deep into the heart of a man or woman. Sometimes this crack starts even before we can talk. One or both parents may have abandoned us. We could have been put up for adoption. We could have lost our parents to death or divorce. Regardless of how or why abandonment occurs, the pain is real.

Sometimes we don't trust or let others into our hearts. Sometimes we use anger or a set of diversion behaviors to aid us with abandonment. Diversion behaviors include overinvolvement in activities, relationships, or causes. This overactivity keeps the mind too busy to stop, feel, and process pain.

For others, diversions can be a constant regurgitation of negative feelings or focusing on what they don't have or what's wrong with the world. This negative rehearsal also can keep the mind too busy to stop, process, or deal with the real pain. A heart in pain, if it is not actively healing, will create some sort of distraction.

Some spouses continually set themselves up for abandonment. This cycle of abandonment keeps a person chasing love or acceptance, then picking people who won't or can't return their love or acceptance, and then they get hurt and repeat this cycle with the same person or another person all over again.

As with abuse, you can face and heal your abandonment—again, owning (admitting) it, placing the responsibility where it should be, getting counseling if necessary, moving toward forgiveness, and grieving your losses. Symptoms of abandonment issues are:

- An inability to let others into your heart
- Generally not trusting people
- An isolated lifestyle
- An inability to see or accept your flaws
- Focusing on the flaws of others
- Success is feared to be short-lived
- Believing people will leave you
- A general anxiety/insecurity
- Being so successful you don't need anyone

If you find yourself struggling with abandonment, you can attempt to work on this yourself. You can walk through a self-growth process I describe in the book *Get a Grip* (Siloam, 2007). If that is not successful, you may need to try counseling or speaking with someone in the therapeutic ministry in your local area.

It is possible you're reading this section and you think it has some application for your spouse. You can read this section together. If your spouse believes this is an issue, he or she can take the steps we just discussed. If your spouse is unwilling to reach out to heal, then you might consider marriage counseling so you can tackle the problem together.

The Ten-Minute Marriage Principle will help your marriage become stronger; however, if you or your spouse struggles with the wound of abandonment, you may need to apply some extra work to receive the full results you are hoping for. To be more successful in life and to thoroughly enjoy the Ten-Minute Marriage Principle, you'll need to face and process the emotional wound of abandonment.

2. ADDICTIONS

Clem and Marta were happily married for more than thirty years. They had raised their children and enjoyed a pretty affluent lifestyle. Marta believed everything was going great until the day she received "the call." Clem took Marta's car in for repair, so when she needed to go play league tennis that morning, she took Clem's car. She was on her way when the cell phone rang. It wasn't her ringtone, but Clem's. She reached for the phone and smilingly said, "Clem's phone, can I help you?"

The woman on the other end said, "My name is Lily and I have been waiting for Clem to show up. Is he on his way?"

Curious, Marta asked Lily where Clem was to meet her and she said, "He knows—at the club," then hung up.

Marta had a sinking feeling. She quickly checked the number of the person who called and found out it was that of a strip club. She started going through the list of his received calls and found Clem had regularly called and received calls from this number as well as a handful of other strip clubs. Marta frantically started calling the numbers, and all were answered by women who wouldn't give their names but sounded as if they were in their twenties.

Marta's world came tumbling down that day. She confronted Clem and he started to lie, then cry.

Clem had a secret sexual addiction. He was heavily involved in pornography, masturbating, strip clubs, and prostitutes. He had been doing some form of sexual acting out, however, most of their marriage. Clem and Marta came for help and Clem became very serious about his recovery—including taking regular polygraphs to verify that he was no longer participating in these habits.

During the treatment program, it became apparent that Marta also had an addiction. Hers was much more "acceptable," but it was still dangerous: she medicated her emotional pain through spending. She bought things almost daily. She would spend hours tracking down deals. She would travel just to spend. If she felt down, alone, or overwhelmed, she spent money. Because of Clem's guilt about his secret life, he never confronted Marta about her spending.

Addictions often start off in adolescence and early adulthood. They take over more of the person as the person grows. Addictions can be rooted in the spiritual, psychological, or biological part of a person—they can also have tentacles throughout the person. Addicts will deny, lie, and rationalize their addictions for many years as the crack increases in their lives and marriages.

Some use alcohol, drugs, sex, food, or work to escape. Others gamble, exercise, shop, spend, and use the computer or a myriad of other addictions, including relationships. Those struggling with addictions have some common features.

- They have made promises to stop and failed.
- They have faced harmful consequences for the addiction behavior yet continued.
- They show escalated use or practice of the addiction.
- Their vocations or relationships have suffered.
- They show an increased tolerance of the behavior or drug.
- They express denial, minimization, rationalization, or anger when confronted about the addiction.
- Their addiction is often a secret.
- They spend more time, energy, or money pursuing or engaging in the addiction.
- They experience a sense of withdrawal if kept from the addictive behavior.

I have written several books on addiction and recovery and, as an experienced counselor, I know you can heal. You *can* stop the crack in your life and marriage from destroying everything. An addict cannot begin to heal, however, until he or she admits he or she is addicted and asks for help from God and others. Addicts need to attend support groups and seek professionals to discover the roots of their addiction.

Addictions can be kryptonite in a marriage as the spouse begins choosing the addiction over real life and real relationships. The spouse all but disappears from the relationship. The husband or wife's lack of engagement in the marriage and parenting can start cracks in his or her children's lives as well.

At Heart to Heart Counseling Center, we offer Three-Day Intensives for sexual addiction, sexual anorexia, abuse, or abandonment issues as well as Marriage Intensives. For a Three-Day Intensive, a couple comes to our office in Colorado Springs and participates in individual, marital, and group counseling sessions. They also receive educational daily assignments that each spouse must complete independently. Each couple is assigned a specific therapist to address the addiction's impact on both of their lives and the marriage. (For more information, go to our Web site: *www.tenminutemarriage.com*.)

This can be a great way to start recovery. We also have telephone support groups that people find very helpful. Whether you utilize support groups or professional help, reach out. I have seen so many couples walk outside of the grip of addiction and experience incredible marriages once again.

3. SEXUAL ANOREXIA

In seeing couples for over eighteen years, fairly regularly I met with clients who have aggressively avoided intimacy. Over time I put a cluster of symptoms together, and in our field of recovery this condition became known as *intimacy anorexia* or *sexual anorexia*.

Tonya was a very athletic woman who was married to Tim for seventeen years. They had one child. Tonya was a flight attendant and Tim was a chiropractor in a suburb. Tonya worked quite a bit even though she didn't need the money. When Tonya was home, she busied herself with ten-mile runs, swimming, riding her bike, and working out. At night she read books or magazines or studied her Bible. Sex with Tim was infrequent and Tonya never asked for it. Tonya didn't like to pray with Tim, and Tim felt he couldn't connect with Tonya unless they got together to support their child's activities.

Although Tim was fit, he wasn't exactly a calorie counter. He ate burgers now and then and occasionally had a soda or candy bar. Tim reported feeling very alone, but if he and Tonya started getting closer, Tonya regularly picked a fight. Tim felt hopeless about ever feeling loved and felt more like Tonya's servant than her lover or husband.

Micah is an engineer. He and Trisha had been married thirteen years and had two boys. Micah worked a lot. When he came home, he ate and hit the computer for work, watched television, did yard work, or played video games. Micah seemed to be a good dad who was involved in the Boy Scouts with the boys. But Trisha said they didn't really talk. She felt avoided emotionally and spiritually and felt alone even when they had sex.

She tried to suggest marriage books, going to marriage conferences, or even seeking counseling but Micah's response was always the same: "I'm not a girl and I don't do that kind of stuff." Micah controlled Trisha with his cold silence or outbursts of anger. Trisha tried to make the best of their relationship and felt forced by her faith to stay. Micah didn't take any responsibility when he made mistakes in the relationship. Trisha said he blamed her for everything and made her feel needy for wanting a kiss or caress or when she tried to be creative sexually.

We can list some of the symptoms of sexual anorexia:

- Unaffectionate
- Overinvolvement in outside interests
- Never asks for sex; resents being asked for sex
- Starts fights to avoid sex
- Rarely shares intimate feelings or thoughts
- Seems emotionless
- Uses silence, angry outbursts, and shame to control spouse
- Blames spouse for every problem in the marital relationship

Like the food anorexic who refuses to eat, the intimacy or sexual anorexic refuses to connect to his or her spouse. These people can be masterful at other relationships, but in marriage, they avoid intimacy both physical and emotional.

I have put together a checklist so you can see if this is a crack that might be growing in your marriage. You can go to our Website *www.intimatematters.com* to find the nine characteristics of a sexual anorexic. If someone has five or more yes answers, it's probably time to make a call to get help. This crack can be very serious and can largely impact the success of your marriage.

Be careful not to confuse just a bad day or two with intimacy issues or sexual anorexia. This anorexia is a pattern you would see regularly over the marriage.

Intimacy/sexual anorexia is like an addiction. The person who has it can use denial, anger, blaming, or rationalization of the behavior. The intimacy/sexual anorexic can be the nicest man or woman to others. It's only in the marriage that this person avoids intimacy. The spouse of an anorexic feels unimportant, unwanted, and untouched and will feel as if he or she is starving for connection and begging for love.

Persons suffering from intimacy/sexual anorexia can, like other addicts, be helped if they really want to be free. They also have to admit that they have a problem (this is difficult because they desire to be good or seem so most of the time). They have to complete a daily regime of intimacy exercises with their spouses. They also have to initiate sexual intimacy on a regular basis. To be successful early on, they must face consequences for withholding love or sex.

I have had couples so intimacy/sexually anorexic

that they hadn't had sex in more than ten years. After their Three-Day Intensive, these couples were amazingly happy.

I will never forget a Texas man who, two months after he'd been working his treatment plan, sat in my office and cried because he was so happy. He thought he would never be able to intimately connect with the wife he really loved. Healing from intimacy or sexual anorexia is work, but the results are so amazing.

4. ARROGANCE

Here is another kryptonite that can damage a marriage over the years. Arrogance is the belief that you are better or smarter than others, especially your spouse. Arrogance for some starts in childhood or adolescence. Often arrogance is a projection of a bigger self due to pain or fear of the authentic self. The young boy or girl was damaged somehow in his or her heart and now protects that wound with superiority.

Arrogance is kryptonite because it makes intimacy difficult and the relationship chaotic. It's as if arrogant people can't be equal to anyone. Some symptoms of a person with arrogance issues are:

- Every conflict is win or lose; there's no compromise
- Attitude of entitlement
- His or her needs come first
- Not a team player
- Little or no empathy for others

- Uses denial, rationalization, and minimalization to maintain arrogance
- The problem is always someone else's fault

The person suffering from this needs counseling so he or she can understand that imperfection is normal and okay, and the arrogant protection isn't necessary. To heal, this crack, like all the others, requires honesty, acceptance, and support.

Every couple deserves to have an authentic connecting relationship between two flawed but loved people. To have this, both people must accept, not protect, their less-than-wonderful humanity.

As with sexual anorexia, this condition manifests in a regular pattern of behavior. Most of us are guilty of arrogance at some time in our lives, especially in marriage. Who hasn't thought just for a moment that his or her spouse might not be the sharpest knife in the drawer? Then the Holy Spirit corrects our thoughts and we are grateful again to be married to these wonderful persons. If arrogance becomes a habit, though, and a tool for hurting others, seek professional help.

YOU *CAN* QUELL YOUR KRYPTONITE

Any of the kryptonites I've described is something you can walk through and recover from. It may take determination, a clear plan, honesty, and some help from professionals, but you can make progress. I have seen healing from abuse, abandonment, addictions, anorexia, and arrogance happen so often, I know this miracle is possible.

I hope you are encouraged. As I said at the beginning of the chapter, these issues may not be ones you face. They might apply to others you know or friends you haven't met yet. You now have hope and some information to offer other married couples to have a great and maybe even a super marriage!

As you apply your Ten-Minute Marriage Principle, you and your spouse can move closer together than you might have thought possible. The core gets stronger and stronger, and before you know it, the abs of your relationship look like six-pack abs!

Then, as you pick up one support principle after another, the limbs of your relationship are also starting to get stronger. You are starting to look pretty buff in some areas of your relationship. Let's keep going as we work out some more and engage in more support principles to make your marriage look and feel great.

10

THE FORGIVENESS LIFESTYLE

Something that can clog up any marriage is gook. *Gook* refers to those sins and mistakes by which we willfully or unknowingly hurt people. Gook appears in every marriage, Christian or not.

I tell people at marriage conferences that it would be a living hell to be married to a perfect person. Why? Because then all the problems in the marriage would be your fault! As it is, with two sinners married to each other, any issue could be either spouse's fault, or even the fault of both.

In the Ten-Minute Marriage Principle, I am giving you tools to help you have not only a happier marriage but also a more efficient marriage. A marriage with less or managed gook is a much better marriage.

John and Jodi are a great couple, the kind of friends everyone likes to have. They are raising their children right, going to church faithfully, have close friends, and are in good physical health as well. What you don't know is how often they fight. I'm not just talking about how many times a week but how many times they fight about the same things. They report that some of the same arguments go back to their first year of marriage. I know you probably don't know any couples like this . . . but bear with me.

Once they get into one of these arguments, it's as if all their Sunday school lessons go right out the window. When they fight, anything can be said and all of their past history is fair game. What's at the root of John and Jodi's behavior is an *unforgiveness lifestyle*. Their sins against each other stay in big piles, and this eats up a lot of time and emotion in their relationship.

There is another way to live. I call it the *forgiveness lifestyle*. Up front it will cost you some time and effort. Down the road, though, it will save you hundreds of hours of pain and conflict. Imagine just not having some of these conflicts in the future. I live this stuff, so I know it's a sweet alternative to endless bickering and resentment.

Unforgiveness clogs the arteries of life in a relationship the way plaque clogs arteries in the body. In a forgiveness lifestyle, the life flow between the two of you increases. You may work a little hard over the next few pages, but I encourage you to do this so you can have a healthy, growing marriage.

YOU FIRST

"You first" is a polite saying we use when two people intersect at a door at the same time. "You first" can be what you say to your companion when the waitress comes to your table to take your order. "You first" is also the best first step in the forgiveness lifestyle.

You might have heard some preaching on loving others as you love yourself. The way some people love themselves isn't to be wished on others! The fact is, you can't love or forgive others if you can't love or forgive yourself. So as I said, "You first."

In this chapter, we will move quite quickly to maximize your results. I strongly encourage both of you to do the exercises presented in this chapter to achieve the greatest results. I have assisted many couples who were bitter and unforgiving in adopting a forgiveness lifestyle.

You, too, might experience what many of my clients have as they have walked through these principles together: they felt lighter, they could breathe more easily, they felt rejuvenated—like after recovering from an illness.

All of us make some mistakes, after all, that is part of the journey of life. When we think of forgiveness, we often think about how others have made mistakes against us. But too often we neglect the mistakes or sins we have committed against others or ourselves. Sinning against ourselves can also cause us pain or woundedness that we need to address to live a forgiveness lifestyle.

The work we are about to do is good for the soul and for the marriage. So get ready to feel lighter and freer than ever before!

On a piece of paper, make a list of how you have sinned against yourself. Here is a list of possible entries:

- Not listening to what is right
- Not taking care of my body
- Sexual behavior before marriage
- Angry outbursts
- Abortions
- Pornography
- Self-deception
- Grandiosity
- Not valuing myself
- The way I treat my family, friends, or children

Now that you have made your own list, let me give you some options people have found helpful to do with their list of mistakes toward themselves. Once they've listed their sins against themselves, some clients do something symbolic to express forgiveness and to let go of these sins.

Cynthia, a single twenty-four-year-old, had made some serious mistakes in her past. She used some drugs, had premarital sex, and felt really guilty about some of the relationship choices she had made. She decided to write them all down on separate pieces of paper, blow up balloons, and insert the papers in them. She then went to the beach and confessed each of the sins out loud, saying something like, "I agree with Jesus to forgive myself for _____." She went through each one of the sins she had committed toward herself.

Kirk was married and forty-seven. He lived in Colorado, so the great outdoors was a big part of his life. He also wrote out a list of sins he had committed against himself, such as anger, self-hatred, poor vocational and relationship choices, and how he let himself down as a dad and husband. He then placed each of the sins from his list on an index card.

He took his stack of cards to a mountain about an hour from where he lived. He was all alone in the middle of nowhere. He said a prayer in which he forgave himself for each sin. He then dug a hole in the ground, placing the cards in it. He covered the hole with dirt and a rock. He committed to leave what was buried under the rock at the cross.

Angelique wanted to do something different with her list. She was a thirty-two-year-old married woman who worked full-time as an accountant. To deal with her list, she stayed home one morning as her husband and girls went to a soccer game. She said she would catch up with them in a little while.

Angelique took her list of sins and walked into the guest room in the house, which contained a full-length mirror. She stood facing the mirror and asked herself for forgiveness: "Angelique, I have sinned against you by _____. Would you forgive me?" After she mentioned each of her sins, she then looked herself in the eye and said, "I forgive you." This took a little time, but she was able to get through the entire list. After she completed her self-forgiveness, she took the list, ripped it up in little pieces, and put it in a Baggie.

On her way to the soccer game, she stopped by a fast-food restaurant and put the Baggie of all her sins in a garbage can. She went to the game and her daughters' team won—but she felt she had also won that day.

I mentioned the empty-chair exercise in my books *Intimacy: A 100-Day Guide to Lasting Relationships* and *The 7 Love Agreements*. Some find this a helpful method for self-forgiveness as well. Here, instead of a mirror, you just place a chair in front of you and ask forgiveness from yourself, then move to the other chair to grant forgiveness to yourself.

Regardless of how creative you are in the process of forgiving yourself, it is very important that you have three basic elements involved in your process:

1. A written list of your sins
2. Verbally expressed forgiveness
3. A place in time when you know you have completed this process

Those Who've Sinned Against You

In Genesis 2:21, God took the rib from Adam to make woman. The verse says He "closed up the place with flesh." That's interesting to me. God didn't want to give Eve a wounded man. He didn't want their relationship to start off from a wounded place.

Most of us have had people hurt us deeply—perhaps parents, friends, siblings, people with whom we've had romantic relationships, or even former spouses. For others, these hurts may include sexual abuse, rape, or other significant traumas. (Note: For those who have experienced trauma, I recommend you e-mail my office at heart2heart@xc.org. I have an exercise called Cleansing the Temple that can facilitate healing.)

Now we are going to talk about how to practice a forgiveness lifestyle when someone else has wounded you. Some spend many years running away from dealing with their wounds. I would rather run toward this place. It's much faster to address a wound when you're running toward it.

Be brave and be focused as we turn the following pages. You can definitely experience some growth as you add this support principle to your Ten-Minute Marriage Principle.

Again, you will need to make a list. With this list in hand, you will need to forgive each person. Some people do this by speaking it out loud. Some go to a quiet location and process this alone, in silence. Some write out the offense and then write out the forgiveness (if you do this, read the letters out loud). You may feel more comfortable doing this with a counselor or pastor in the same room.

Regardless of how you express forgiveness of others, you need the three specific elements:

1. A written list
2. A method to verbally forgive
3. A time when you know you have completed the forgiveness

On a sheet of paper, complete this list of the people who have sinned against you (do not include your spouse on this list—we'll cover him or her in a later exercise). Then make a note of the specific sin that each person committed against you.

Remember, forgiveness is a gift you give to yourself. This gift allows you to disconnect from the perpetrator and the pain and release them from your heart so you can heal.

You see, the less your heart is walled off with the gook of unforgiveness, the stronger and healthier it can be. By going through these exercises, I and many others have experienced such a release of pain. This allows us to be more gracious to the persons who sinned against us.

If my heart has less gook, it can be more alive to love my wife, Lisa, and my children. Even my dog, Moses, gets a little more grace if I can live a forgiveness lifestyle of letting go of the past!

YOUR SPOUSE'S SINS AGAINST YOU

It's true, you married a sinner. Even the one who walked down the aisle with you and promised to love you has, at some point, sinned against you. Some of those sins will be small and some will be . . . let's just say "bigger."

Some of those sins are more consistent than other sins. Some sins are absolutely accidental, unintentional, and done unknowingly. Other sins are not accidents. They are intentional and sometimes your spouse's intent was to hurt you. Yes, this does happen in most marriages.

So, as you did with yourself and others, make a list of these sins, be they behaviors, actions, or attitudes. One word of caution: *under no circumstances are you to show this list to your spouse.* This forgiveness exercise is for you, regardless of your spouse's awareness. Just as you have unknowingly sinned against your spouse, so has your spouse sometimes unknowingly sinned against you.

Just as we talked about previously, you will need to have the same three elements in this exercise to forgive your spouse.

1. A written list
2. A verbal response
3. A definite time when you know you have forgiven
   your husband or wife

You may not be able to forgive all of the sins you listed right away. Be honest about this. Some of the items may even fall into the trauma category (i.e., physical or verbal abuse, neglect, adultery, or marital rape). If so, do the Cleansing the Temple exercise so you can more fully heal before you attempt the forgiveness exercise, or seek competent counseling.

As you live the forgiveness lifestyle, you will find that granting forgiveness comes much more easily, even if your spouse doesn't ask for it.

YOUR SINS AGAINST YOUR SPOUSE

We have addressed the possible sins that others have committed against you as well as sins you've committed against yourself. This is hard work, and I congratulate you if you are completing the various forgiveness exercises. If you have, you have lost some unforgiveness that may have been clogging up your life and your marriage.

Now I want discuss how to deal with the sins you have committed against someone else—specifically, your spouse. I know I still sin, though I really hate to. You know the feeling when your words or attitudes hurt those you love the most. It's time to address this yucky pile of gook that could be clogging up the marriage from your end.

You may be thinking, *I hope he is not thinking what I think he is thinking*. You're right. I am thinking what you think I'm thinking.

It's time to get out that tablet and pen. This time you will list your sins in the marriage. You will start with your dating days and work to the present, listing the sins in both attitude and action you have committed in this relationship. Be rigorously honest. (These are only sins you haven't confessed to God and/or the person yet.) Get them down on paper.

You may need to ask God to help you recall your sin history. Some of us struggle with sin amnesia: you know, we forget our sins but remember all the sins of others. I find this syndrome prevalent, so be prayerful.

Be mindful of the sins in which you failed to do something, such as praising your spouse, touching him or her, listening, saying "I love you," or initiating intimacy. These are hurtful "inactions," so to speak.

List your active sins in one column and your "inactive" sins in the next column. It should look like this:

I sinned by doing	*I sinned by not doing*

Do a good job on your sin list. I want you to experience a lifestyle of total forgiveness, and this includes both forgiving others and regularly asking forgiveness for your own sins when you commit them.

You might be thinking, *All right, I'll make my list and maybe role-play my spouse forgiving me.* No, that won't work. Remember James 5:16: "Confess your sins to each other and pray for each other so that you may be healed. The prayer of a righteous man is powerful and effective."

When you've finished your list, make an appointment with your spouse. You need to prepare your husband or wife for what you want to do. Ask these questions, which will draw safe and healthy boundaries around your conversation:

1. I would like to talk to you about some mistakes I made in our relationship. Do you have about an hour to do this with me?
2. I need you to listen fully to me without asking questions. Can you do this?
3. When I ask you to forgive me for something I only need you to say, "I forgive you" or that you need more time. I will be too vulnerable at that moment to hear any other comments. Can you agree to this?
4. After I go over this list with you, I need you not to bring up anything on this list for at least seventy-two hours. Can you do this?

If you don't think your spouse has this level of self-control, do this exercise in the presence of a pastor or counselor. Note: before confessing infidelity your spouse doesn't know about, seek the advice of a pastor or counselor, and make sure you invite such a third party to sit in on the confession. Your spouse will need support in hearing such devastating news, and he or she may not know how to respond to it.

If your spouse can't agree to these boundaries, don't proceed. Then, if your spouse can be approached in the future, try again. If your spouse is unwilling to work through this exercise with you, you might need to use the symbolic empty-chair or face-a-mirror method. But, if at all possible, do it face-to-face. Both you and your spouse can experience connection and healing in this process.

This exercise is to help you get the gook out. If you and your spouse want to do this exercise together, great! Set a time. Be sure to stay totally focused on your sins even if you believe your spouse's sin list is bigger than yours.

ONE MORE TO GO!

I really wish my spouse was the only person I sinned against. Unfortunately, my sinful nature can manifest on almost anyone. I can be unloving, arrogant, irritable, rude, and self-centered to almost anyone, even the people I like or love.

Like me, you've sinned against others throughout your life. To live a forgiveness lifestyle, you need to do another rigorous self-examination of your sins toward others.

I know this is uncomfortable. I didn't like doing this

exercise either! But I made a list of employers, parents, and professors—everyone I could think of—and yes, I went back to every person and asked for forgiveness. Initially I felt odd doing this, but afterward I felt great!

What this process gave me was freedom from shame and guilt. I no longer was ashamed of any hurts I caused others. I can run into anyone from my past and keep my head up. Once I owned the junk from my past, I could get rid of it.

I caution you, though: I strongly discourage you from going directly to an ex-love for forgiveness. Revisiting a previous lover is never a great idea for a married person. You can stir up old feelings, reignite attachments, compare that person's strengths to your spouse's weaknesses, or hurt your ex-love's life with your interruption. You should never attempt fresh communication with a former love without the direction of a counselor. Also, if your confession could cause legal issues or significant pain because the person doesn't know you sinned against him or her, consult a pastor or counselor for guidance before attempting this.

Better yet, leave the past love in the past and use the empty-chair method of asking for and receiving forgiveness. This way you get to own—and release—your mistakes without risking a potentially damaging encounter.

If you are brave enough to ask forgiveness for past sins, you can clean up any clogs you have in relationships. This makes you lighter in your soul and much easier to live with. The humility this adds to your life can be a lifelong gift. This process also allows you to be more honest about your sins.

For me, asking for forgiveness is as easy as saying "Thank you." I know I need to do this regularly, so I am prepared. I have learned to apologize quickly to my wife, children, myself, my staff, coworkers, clients, business associates, and others I come in contact with. I am not perfect, and apologizing regularly reminds me of this fact.

Knowing I need forgiveness myself allows me to forgive my wife and others I love. I know I am going to do my best to forgive even when no one asks for it. This helps me continue to love on days when I would rather build a wall of unforgiveness. This lifestyle helps me personally maintain living the Ten-Minute Marriage Principle. I don't have to keep bringing up Lisa's past or respond out of shame to my past. When we do our exercises, there's no silent resentment building up, so we can be honestly loving toward one another. That alone is worth the work I have had to do in the area of forgiveness.

Make a Note

I liken seeking forgiveness to climbing a mountain. If I am going to do something difficult, it is helpful to have checkpoints along the way so I can mark my progress. If checkpoints are helpful to you as well, take a sheet of paper and make a Forgiveness Checklist. List the person you forgave or who forgave you as well as the date each occurred. You'll have a visual record of the work you've done.

I encourage you to schedule a few minutes a day

or a half hour a week to work on this. As you get rid of the gook, all of life will be more beautiful! As you complete one forgiveness process, move to the next. You will grow stronger as you climb this mountain. As you climb, keep in mind the view you will have for yourself, your spouse, and others: somehow you will be different, more grounded and grateful than you were before you climbed.

I want to leave you hopeful that if you climb the mountain of forgiveness, your life and your marriage will change. Sometimes when our family goes hiking, the difficulty of the trail makes us want to give up, but if we climb just a little farther, the panoramic view we experience is absolutely incredible.

So go ahead: climb, see, and breathe a new lifestyle. Forgive, and you'll feel and be freer than ever before.

11

THE TEN-MINUTE TEAM

Marriage is a team sport. Many married people charge into marriage believing that their love can and will solve anything: *It's us against the world*. When you are young and more naive, these ideals almost seem to work, at least for a while. Then life throws you some circumstances that are bigger than the two of you.

I want to show you a real team approach to marriage. By the end of this chapter I hope you'll clearly see the need for a team of people to consult, put a team together, and know how to contact these people within ten minutes' time. When you are able to do this, you have created a Ten-Minute Team for your marriage.

Why is this important? Because when you need help, you usually need it right away. Crises give you very little warning. If you can gather the experts you need in minutes, you can get immediate feedback on the circumstance you face. Each team member has his or her function. Combining these strengths makes you a formidable opponent to crisis.

Suppose you are clicking along, faithfully doing

your exercises as you live out the Ten-Minute Marriage Principle. You and your spouse are experiencing a real connection on a daily basis. You, your marriage, even your children seem to be doing life better.

Then it happens. There's no telling what it could be. It could be a call about an accident, disease, even a death of a family member or friend. It could be a personal or financial crisis for you, your spouse, children, extended family, or a friend. It could even be a positive thing like suddenly selling a piece of property. A really positive "crisis" could also be your son going to state for his sport in two weeks. You may be happy about the event itself, but the extra demands on your time are stressful.

These events, positive or not, will impact your marriage. How severely, and how long, they will impact it can largely depend on whether you have developed your team.

Let me give you a quick example. I have a friend who is very successful in his industry. He and I get together periodically and chat about all kinds of topics. He has elected to put me on his Ten-Minute Team. So occasionally I'll get the call saying, "Doug, I need your help with something."

Most times I get this call when he is at a loss on how to handle a relationship issue, be it with his wife, employees, or someone he is helping. We chat about it for a little while and he says, "Thanks a lot." He goes back to face his situation empowered and with some new ideas and life goes on. If he hadn't reached out to someone, he would have been trapped within his own ideas and maybe not have solved the situation as well or as early.

Becoming better equipped for crisis will help you practice the Ten-Minute Marriage Principle because you won't be distracted when difficulties arise. You'll have time and energy to devote to improving your relationship even as you face a difficult situation.

THE NUMBER-ONE TEAM MEMBER: GOD

The most important team member you will have is God. He is all-knowing and all-powerful, a creative God who loves you and your spouse. And God is impartial in disputes where you may have different opinions on a matter.

Seek God daily. You can find Him in His Word, the Bible. You can find Him in prayer with your spouse and individually. You can find Him through your pastor or spiritual director, and you can find Him when you just stop and worship Him. Couples who regularly seek God and make marriage a union of three face life's special circumstances much better than those who leave God at the church building.

God is a person; He definitely has feelings for people and standards of behavior for them to practice. If you are a parent, suppose you had two adult children, say two girls. One of your sons-in-law disrespects your daughter, doesn't involve you in their family, and personally avoids you. It turns out he really misrepresented who he was when he married your daughter. The other son-in-law really does love your other daughter. He treats her and you with respect, he involves you in their lives together, and he seeks out time with you so he can deepen his relationship with you.

Which of these sons-in-law would you favor? Of course, the one who really loves your child. He loves the person you love. When someone loves the person you love, you favor that person. Look over the life of your child. Think about those teachers, coaches, activity leaders, and church leaders who loved your children: aren't those people you appreciated and respected?

I know this is true for Lisa and me. We love our children's pastors. We also love the couple who ran the Easter play Hadassah and Jubal took part in this year. Lisa and I find it easy to love those who love our kids.

I believe much of the favor of God in my life exists because of how I love the persons God loves, especially my wife. Am I perfect? No. But I try, and I faithfully bring Lisa to her Father on a daily basis. God knows I love Lisa, but I think He really likes our "visiting" Him together.

If you are not sensing God's love and favor, it may be because you've grown estranged from your Father. As part of living the Ten-Minute Marriage Principle, you may need to choose exercises that develop you spiritually as a couple. You can be creative on how you involve God in your marriage.

Take a fresh sheet of paper and finish this sentence:

I/we will make God a part of my/our marital team by _____.

THE LOCAL CHURCH

Many of us know God as our Father. One of the things He encourages in order for the team to be strong and prepared is quality family time: being involved in a local church. In my church, we are encouraged to read the Scriptures, become what God wants us to be, and serve each other and the community.

Why is family time so important? Here are three reasons.

1. CHURCH KEEPS YOU AND YOUR SPOUSE GROWING SPIRITUALLY

You know how you can say something to your spouse and he or she won't hear it, but when someone else— particularly a spiritual authority you both respect—says that same thing, your spouse hears it? As you grow together spiritually, you can become better spouses.

I think we all would like our spouses to be more spiritual. I mean, we all need more kindness, love, patience, and grace. So as we both grow, we have extra spiritual resources with which to do marriage and life together. This will also enhance your practicing the Ten-Minute Marriage Principle—when you have more love to give, your relationship can only improve!

2. CHURCH GIVES YOU FRIENDS WITH SIMILAR VALUES

Not everyone in church is in the same place you are, but you can usually find some people with whom you have enough in common that you can grow in your marriages and families together.

3. CHURCH GIVES YOU A PLACE TO SERVE

You know that as a family, you're a team for helping each other out—but this should also include people outside the family. Service is part of being in the family of God.

When my daughter was six years old, she heard our pastors tell her everybody has a ministry and can serve. She asked to serve, but at that time the children's department wasn't ready for an eager six-year-old. That didn't stop Hadassah. She, with Jubal and the rest of the family, found that a person of any age could help make sandwiches.

Let me explain, because not every church has a ministry to make sandwiches! In our church, we reach out to the special-needs people in our community. They are bused in from all over the city to come to church and then receive a meal. That meal consists of sandwiches, among other items. Hadassah found out that any age person could put sandwiches together. So the Weiss family is pretty good at making quality mass-produced sandwiches on Sunday morning. Because of Hadassah's desire to serve her bigger church family, all of us serve where she and Jubal do. Today they do this as well as help in the children's department. They understand that when you're part of a family, you have a place to serve.

My mother-in-law was a great example of this. She had six children, a husband, and an immaculate house.

She served her local church her entire life, in the nursery, office, and prayer meetings. When she recently went to heaven, hundreds of people flew from all over the country to pay their respects. At the viewing, acquaintances said again and again how this woman's life touched them. She loved her family and she loved her church family.

Go serve and see the benefits in others' lives and your own. No matter how old or young you are, in a healthy local church you can find a place to serve and be a blessing to others. As you make this a lifestyle, you begin to put a stop to the "it's all about me" American attitude. Then we will be more selfless in our lives and in our marriages.

I am a strong supporter of couples' finding and committing to a local church. Lisa and I have never left a church without the pastors' and elders' blessing and confirming that it was God who was moving us to another church.

Some couples miss this basic ingredient in their marriages and families. I know that there are unhealthy, controlling, showboat churches that are dysfunctional. Don't use them as an excuse for your not finding a healthy church in which to grow your marriage and family. It's out there!

God is an amazing being. He does, however, allow us to team up with several others to navigate this thing called marriage. On your piece of paper, finish this sentence:

I/we will make the church a part of my/our marriage team by _____.

PASTORS OR SPIRITUAL LEADERS:
MORE TEAM MEMBERS

Having a pastor or spiritual leader as a teammate for your marriage is a really good idea. Jesus related to us the idea that God's people are like sheep. You know, sheep have no natural defense mechanisms. They are not fast, aggressive, or even all that intelligent in matters of self-preservation. In fact, without shepherds, sheep can get into all kinds of peril.

Since becoming a Christian, I have always had a pastor as part of my team, even before I was married. In twenty years of marriage, Lisa and I have had several pastors guide us in our relationship.

My experience is that pastors have a way of seeing me differently than I see myself—usually better, or at least more honestly. In major decisions, I always include the input of my pastor. I want to know what he, as part of my team, thinks. Our pastor's perspective and encouragement have greatly strengthened my life and our marriage.

If you have a pastor or spiritual leader you trust, invite him or her to be part of your marital team. If you don't know such a person yet, I strongly encourage you to look for a spiritual leader whose life, marriage, and leadership you respect. This is something you should do early in your relationship rather than when you are in crisis.

Finish one of the next two sentences:

My/our spiritual leaders' names are _____
_____.

If I/we don't have a spiritual leader teammate, my/our plan is _____.

Extended Family as Part of the Team

That's right; extended family can also be part of your marriage team. Actually, whether we like it or not, and whether we ask them or not, family members often feel they are part of our team and express their opinions all the time to prove it!

1. PARENTS

The key family members are both sets of parents. Obviously every couple faces a unique combination of personalities in their inherited family. Some in-laws are very spiritual, mature people who always want what is best for the both of you. They love and listen to you both during important discussions. In some families, the in-laws can be spiritually and emotionally immature. They may have a long history of bad decisions. They may want to talk only with their child, not the both of you. They might also be thinking about what is best for them rather than for you in some circumstances.

One thing that family offers is a history of knowing us. They know some of the life lessons we've learned. Our parents have seen our lives from the very beginning. They can, in a kind or sometimes more forthright way, remind us of our histories.

Here is where a team concept can be helpful. If you invite your parents to be part of your team, to talk to you honestly when you ask for input, they can be incredibly helpful. They need to understand that they are just part of the team, though, and not the only people you seek information from. All team members weigh in on matters that we are asking them for their help on. In other words, no one person or one couple is going to tell you what to do; you rely on all of the team to guide you to wise decisions. As team members, your parents should expect to be heard but not necessarily "obeyed."

When you set these ground rules with your family members, you can avoid hard feelings. If parents think you're asking them as parents, not team members, for advice, when you don't comply they might offer all kinds of negative thoughts. As part of a team, they shouldn't be offended if your other team members have different opinions. This can make differences of opinion with parents resolve smoothly over the course of your marriage.

As a counselor, I know that it's not possible to have a healthy relationship with some people. Some couples' parents are not mature enough even to be teammates. In those situations, you have probably already withdrawn from allowing them to influence your decisions. That is wise.

2. SIBLINGS

If you respect their lifestyles and choices, siblings can also be great consultants on your team. Again, if you invite them, explain that you are utilizing them as *consultants*, especially if they are older siblings.

Siblings can be a great asset especially in asking

more questions. They are usually close to the same age as you and your spouse. They come from the same culture and have friends who might have faced the same issues. If your siblings also have healthy marriages, they can be an enormous help.

For some people, neither side of the family has what you would consider great teammates for your marriage. In that case, you might consider adopting some older, mentor-type couples to help fill this gap in your team.

On your piece of paper, finish the first two sentences. If neither applies to you, finish the third sentence.

Our parental team members are _____
_____.

Our sibling team members are _____
_____.

If our families can't serve as team members, we plan to ask _____ to be mentors to us.

FRIENDS

Friends can be very important members on your Ten-Minute Team, and they don't have to be local to be helpful. Friend teammates can be long-distance, people who have known you for years. Lisa, my wife, has such a friend whom she's known since elementary school. When they get together, it's as if time and distance never existed. If Lisa needs to chat about life, herself, the children, or me, she knows she has a listening ear and loving advice always available.

Some of you have friends like this. Usually, though, friends come and go in our lives. These seasons of friendships are very real and fulfilling, even if they're temporary. Whatever the length of the relationship, I find my friends, like siblings, are stellar at asking me questions. Their investigation of the issue or my heart on the issue can lead me to the right answer.

A group of my guy friends and I were talking when one of the men asked for advice on an investment. After a healthy interaction, he was clear on what he should do. Funny enough—it was what his wife had told him in the first place!

Friends come in three major categories.

1. COUPLE FRIENDS

First, there are couple friends. The four of you get along together. You go out to dinner and invite each other over, and everyone seems to be connected and comfortable with one another.

Often these friends are at least unofficially part of your team anyway. You glean from each other on how to live life well, differently, or with more fun. You find yourself discussing personal issues without fear of embarrassment.

If you don't officially have such people as teammates, take your piece of paper and write out names of couples who might be part of your team. Also write down the names of some people you want to get to know as potential friends and team members.

Our current couple friends and potential teammates are

_____.

Our potential friends and teammates are _____

_____.

2. HIS FRIENDS

The second category is the husband's friends. That's right, men having male friends is important to a healthy marriage. Don't go overboard here—if you're spending more time with your friends than with your wife, you are hurting your marriage and family.

That being said, having friends to hang out with, pray with, and talk to is important. Guys don't get together and have tea to talk. We set up events, golf, basketball, adventures, or food and then somewhere along the way, we talk. We talk about family, work, sports, the dog, and stuff like cars, so a lot of it is not touchy-feely.

But it's important to be honest with a couple of guys about how you're doing. Accountability and honesty are great ways to protect yourself, your marriage, and your family from pain. Men need men to stay men. Men think very differently from their wives. They usually don't pull punches and their questions are often more direct.

I realize that men's friendships can be seasonal. Men can lose and need to replace male friends. This can be as simple as making a list of potential guy friends you would like to connect with and inviting them to get together. If you share a mutual interest and know how to reciprocate in a relationship, then you've found some potential teammates. These men may or may not be aware that they are your teammates, but you will know if you want to utilize them in this way in your life.

I strongly encourage men to have a few guys they stay connected to. This is great for their lives and for their marriages. Husband, on your piece of paper, finish the next two sentences:

My positive male friends and potential teammates are

_____.

My future friend possibilities are _____

_____.

3. THE WIFE'S FRIENDS

Women need to get together and share. They also glean from each other's successes and mistakes in life. Ladies also need encouragement to keep being great wives, mothers, daughters, and sisters. Women with close friends do much better in life and in marriage.

Ladies getting together can look totally different from men getting together, but they still talk about the issues in their lives. Women are good at connecting emotionally. Women ask great questions of the heart, and they know how to laugh. I know when Lisa gets together with her girlfriends, she has a good time. It's a totally different good time than guys have together. Lisa needs these breathers of connecting and enjoying her friends. She comes back happier and refreshed to take on all of what being a wife and mother demands of her.

Guys, it's really helpful for you to support your wife here. Sometimes you may have to choose a night once a week or every other week that is your wife's night out. Years ago I had to work hard to convince Lisa to do this, but now she just lets me know when I get to have my children here and there so she can go out and have a good time.

The myth is that every woman knows how to take time for herself. Over the years I have met women who have so isolated themselves in their worlds of responsibility that they have lost their precious friends.

Wife, go ahead and make a list similar to your husband's. Then call and try to get together with some people on the list. Like your husband's friends, they may not know you are utilizing them in this way, but it's inevitable that you will glean from and be helped by them.

My female friends and potential teammates are _____ _____.

My potential female friends/teammates could be _____ _____.

PROFESSIONALS

Marriage is an area where having a few competent professionals on your team can save so much wear and tear in your relationship. Again, you want these teammates on board before you need them. You can then consult these professionals whenever you need their particular expertise.

These are not necessarily people you "invite" to be part of your team, but they're people you need to know you can call if a crisis occurs. Three kinds (at least) are important.

1. A FINANCIAL TEAMMATE

You will need financial counsel throughout your marriage. Eventually you'll have to proactively address making large purchases, college funds, retirement, and other issues. Enlisting a competent accountant or financial planner is critical to marital health and growth.

You will probably have financial conflict sometime in your marriage. You can fight with each other for hours, days, or weeks, or you can consult a wise team member who is familiar with your situation to help you find resolution. Even in a phone call or a short meeting, financial team members can bring clarity to a decision or discussion. Sometimes just a few minutes with such a teammate means Lisa and I get to a decision without any fuss at all.

If you have never added these people to your marital team, brainstorm about who might be helpful. If you don't know any potential financial teammates, write out your plan to locate some in the future.

Our financial teammates are _____

_____.

Our plan for getting financial teammates is _____

_____.

2. A MEDICAL TEAMMATE

Lisa and I are blessed to have a pharmacist as a brother-in-law, a nurse as Lisa's friend, and a very competent doctor we respect. Medical issues are a stressful part of marriage and family. Medical teammates are very helpful in a crisis. When you, the children, or others you care about have a medical emergency, you want to consult persons you trust.

Finish these sentences on your piece of paper.

Our medical teammates are _____

_____.

Our plan to find medical teammates is _____

_____.

3. A COUNSELOR TEAMMATE

You may never need one, but often when you do, you have little time to locate one. Your marriage may be in the best shape possible today, but you never know what will happen to challenge your relationship.

Having a professional counselor who shares your values can be critical during an emotional crisis of any kind. Ask for recommendations from your spiritual leaders, friends, or family. You can ask these potential teammates a few questions and list their numbers in the phone book for future reference—for you or someone else.

Take a few minutes to think about who these people might be.

Our counselor is _____

_____.

Our plan to locate a counselor is _____

_____.

YOUR TEAM

Let's see how well balanced your team is today. Below, just check the boxes for those you feel are established parts of your team.

- ☐ God
- ☐ Pastor/Spiritual Leader
- ☐ Family
    - ☐ His Parents
    - ☐ Her Parents
    - ☐ Siblings
    - ☐ Mentor Couple
- ☐ Friends
    - ☐ Our Friends
    - ☐ His Friends
    - ☐ Her Friends
- ☐ Professionals
    - ☐ Financial
    - ☐ Medical
    - ☐ Counselor

As you look at the boxes you didn't mark off, you can see where you need to do some work. You deserve to enjoy a loving, lasting marital relationship! Having a team can make your dream of a great marriage more of a reality.

Walking through marriage with others means you face problems with more ideas, solutions, and laughter. Your marriage can be about you two, or you can open your hearts to others. I strongly recommend a team concept.

Your living the Ten-Minute Marriage Principle can definitely be strengthened by the utilization of a team. Instead of relying upon each other to meet all the needs a team should meet, you and your spouse can take pressure off yourselves. This frees you up to keep improving your relationship.

A team can also help strengthen your marriage at critical moments. Their assured counsel and ready advice can guide you through the most difficult situations you face. If your marriage is already stronger because of the Ten-Minute Marriage Principle lifestyle, when you get hit with a crisis, a team will help maintain that strength. You can reach out to your team members and very quickly become calm and grounded, focused and able to start navigating the course of this crisis.

As you include team members in your marriage, you will reduce the conflict and increase the joy in your relationship. Team members who share the load make the journeys not shorter but more fun. Happy trails!

12

GO OUT!

Norman and Betty were the loveliest couple you could meet. They served their community and church regularly. They had two children in junior high who were active in sports, choir, and youth groups. Sometimes for Norman and Betty—and you may relate to this—the weekends were harder on them than the workweek!

Norman loved his job and Betty loved her life of raising the children, volunteering, going to Bible studies, and having friends over. Norman and Betty had a strong marriage, but something was slowly starting to strain their love for each other.

They found that they were bickering about small issues on a regular basis. Although they prided themselves on being each other's best friend, they increasingly found themselves not liking each other. One day when they were getting into a snit, Norman cursed at Betty, something he hadn't done for decades. Betty was hurt and that's when they decided to stop in my office— "Before things get worse," they said.

After meeting Norman and Betty, I started with the

concept of going out. "So how often do you two go on dates with each other?" Betty and Norman looked at each other, then back at me. This is usually not a good sign. It's as if they were each hoping the other could come up with an idea. They each mentioned a few instances, but then the other countered that a child, friend, or couple was involved in those occasions.

After a while, Norman and Betty concluded that their last date had occurred about nine months before. "That's a considerable time not to have gone out together and just been alone with each other," I commented. They agreed and were surprised that this had slipped their attention. It turns out the lack of going out was the source of friction.

WHY DATING IS VITAL TO YOUR RELATIONSHIP

Why is this? You see, when you get married, intuitively you sign up to have fun. You know there will be some responsibility, but really you think there will also be some fun involved. After all, it took you all these years to find your ultimate playmate, your spouse!

That was my idea when I married Lisa. Actually that's one of the things I love and loved about Lisa. She enjoys doing a broad range of things. And she was as beautiful riding a horse, bicycling, getting all dolled up to go to the theater, or just going, in jeans and a T-shirt, to a coffee shop.

I loved dating Lisa and all the long walks and talks we had together. Countless times we just sat in her car for hours, talking. You probably have similar memories from dating your husband or wife. Remember the smiles, relaxed attitude, dreams, brilliance that attracted you to each other? I'll bet that at the time, you were projecting to your future spouse that you were and would be fun as well!

What happened to Norman and Betty happens to so many couples as they go through the various stages of marriage. Before children, many couples still go out on dates. They have fun, are creative, and don't think getting together takes too much effort.

It's the next stage of the marriage where couples begin to struggle with prioritizing dates. You guessed it: the arrival of the first, second, and/or third child. The couple is thrown into parenthood, and they're coping with sleepless nights, long days, and working hard to try to afford that larger apartment, first house, and probably bigger or safer car.

Those early child-rearing years are a critical period in which dating can fall by the wayside just because of time constraints. That is the stage Norman and Betty were in, where couples lose sight of the importance of maintaining an active dating lifestyle.

As years pass, dating only becomes harder when your kids are in junior high and high school, don't drive yet, and are involved in several activities—sports practices, dances, band. They also have school, dentist appointments, doctors' appointments, birthdays, church events, extended family events—and don't forget holidays and summer vacations.

You can get tired just reading about what parents at this stage of life do! Yet here is where a couple needs going out the most. The demands of life are great, and if a couple isn't careful, they will move into a *functionship* and out of a relationship. In a *functionship*, couples work on completing their to-do lists but not on their relationships. They may eat together, but that's often on the road, quick, and with the kids.

In a *functionship*, both people are prone to burnout, adopt weird eating habits, skip exercise, and feel like members of an assembly line—not like anyone's beloved. In a *functionship*, the Ten-Minute Marriage Principle falls by the wayside as busyness and stress eat up a couple's relationship.

THE DRAMATIC EFFECTS OF DATING

In a relationship, time together has an equal or even higher value than all of this other stuff. In a relationship, make sure that your going-out night is as sacred as your going to church. In this way you enhance your practice of the Ten-Minute Marriage Principle; once again you're committing time to helping your relationship.

Dating was Charles and Betty's area to focus on and they did. They started going out regularly, and within a month, they found their relationship much more fulfilling. The patience they once had with each other was returning. They were having fun again.

Going out, as I've mentioned, is a fundamental aspect to living the Ten-Minute Marriage Principle. If you don't keep oil in an engine, the engine eventually will get hotter and hotter until it's severely damaged. Like a motor, a marriage is a moving entity. Going out is like an oil or lubricant that removes the friction between moving parts so they can operate optimally.

The laughter, chatting, dreaming, or just relaxing together is a great stress release so you can enjoy your Ten-Minute Marriage Principle lifestyle. Marital dating is very helpful for the longevity of your relationship.

If you don't go out, you will eventually spend more time arguing and have to see someone like myself to suggest you start going out again!

A Going-Out Questionnaire

All of us dated prior to marriage. We need to revisit the definition of dating so we can make the most of this support principle in our marriage. After answering these questions, you will be prepared to date successfully for years to come.

How many hours is a date?

2   3   4+

Our answer is: _____.

How often do we want to date?

1 time a week

2 times a month

1 time a month

Our answer is: _____.

What day is best for us to date on?

☐   Monday
☐   Tuesday
☐   Wednesday
☐   Thursday
☐   Friday
☐   Saturday
☐   Sunday

Who is responsible to arrange child care (if applicable)?

☐   He is always
☐   She is always
☐   Whoever is planning the date should do it
☐   Rotate it each date

Who will watch the children (if applicable)?

☐   Oldest child
☐   Paid sitter (adult)
☐   Paid sitter (teen)
☐   Unpaid family member
☐   Friends we rotate with
☐   Other _____

What places are off-limits on a date?

☐ Malls
☐ Wal-Mart
☐ Home Depot
☐ Relatives' homes
☐ _____
☐ _____
☐ _____

What distance will we drive on a date?

☐ Destinations a half hour away
☐ Destinations one hour away
☐ Destinations two hours away
☐ Other_____

What conversation subjects are off-limits on a date?

☐ Sex
☐ Money
☐ Children
☐ Parents
☐ Business (if work together)
☐ Other _____
☐ Other _____

Who chooses a date?

- ☐ He always
- ☐ She always
- ☐ Rotate back and forth

How much can we spend on a date?

$_____

How often can we invite other couples on our date?

- ☐ Anytime
- ☐ Less than 50 percent of the time
- ☐ Less than 25 percent of the time
- ☐ Not at all

What kinds of movies will we watch?

- ☐ PG
- ☐ PG-13 (somewhat sexual)
- ☐ R (action/violence)
- ☐ R (horror)
- ☐ R (sexuality/nudity)

Any other limitations or qualifications for our going out include:

- ☐ _____
- ☐ _____
- ☐ _____
- ☐ _____

A Going-Out Agreement

Now that you have discussed some of the major issues
of going out, let's put it all together. On a sheet of paper,
write out your specific going-out plan. Let me give you
an example from Ray and Megan.

Ray and Megan agree to go out on a three-to-four-hour
date every Tuesday. They chose to rotate responsibility for
their dates. Their child care will be solely Ray's responsibility, and his mother has agreed to watch the children.

Ray and Megan's dates have the limitations of no retail
stores, no conversations about problems of sex or money.
They can spend up to sixty dollars on a date. They can invite
couples less than 25 percent of the time. They limit their
movies to no PG-13 or R-rated movies with nudity or sexual
content and won't drive over an hour one way to any event.

Now it is your turn. Just fill in the blanks as best you
can. Let's start by putting the date on your going-out
agreement.

On this ____ day of _____, 20____, we, _____

_____ (names), agree to a date regularly.

We agree that our date should be approximately _____
hours in length.

_____ is responsible for choosing

activities for our dates. _____ is responsible

for arranging child care, and _____ shall

watch our children.

Our dates have the limitations of _____

_____. We also agree not to have conversa-

tions about _____. We agree to

spend up to $_____ on any given date.

We can invite other couples on our date _____percent
of the time.

We have limited our movie watching to ___-rated movies.

Signed,

_____

_____

    That wasn't so hard! This support principle can add some real fun to your Ten-Minute Marriage Principle lifestyle. As you get closer as a couple, you will have more desire to spend time and have fun together. Lisa and I have had a Going-Out Agreement most of our marriage.

THE CHILDREN

Parents' going out regularly is also very healthy for their children. A mom and dad who want to be together, forsaking all others—including the children—to connect and make sure they stay in love send a very healthy message to their kids. Children need to know their parents prize one another above all else. They don't feel abandoned because of your date. They look forward to having someone else to play with!

In his eleven years, my son has never asked to go along on a date with us. My daughter asked one time when she was about two or three and has never asked since, and she is now thirteen. When I have asked my children, "How do you know I love your mother?" our going out is one of the items they always list.

My children are learning how to be married by how Lisa and I live together. If we had a marriage that did not include regular going out, I'm sure they wouldn't think it was fun to get and stay married. Going out allows Lisa and me to get refreshed, which makes us better parents. We are more able to celebrate and serve our children. Due to our going-out lifestyle, being parents doesn't burn us out or replace our relationship with each other.

So not only is your going out good for your children because it makes them feel secure about their parents' marriage, it also gives them better parents. If you have not been going out because you think it is somehow not good for the children, think again, and start your going-out lifestyle.

If you do this, you will be creating many positive memories for your marriage. This support principle definitely adds vigor to your marriage. What good would it be to have a body that's in great shape but incapable of having fun? You might have met someone like that, but he or she was much too serious. For me, part of staying physically healthy is so that I can keep having fun with my wife and family.

Marriage is some work, but also it is a lot of fun. Going out keeps the fun quotient high and reminds you why you wanted to get married in the first place.

IDEAS

All right, you're ready to go out now. Next I want to share some ways to increase your repertoire of going-out ideas.

The first thing you can do is to ask others who are going out, be they married or single. This is a great question to ask in a social setting. After you get past the few jokes ("Dating—what's that?"), you can usually get some good ideas flowing.

You can also go on Amazon.com or to a bookstore to check out a few dating books. Reading one of these can help you find things you might like to do. You can check the Web site for your local chamber of commerce (or those of nearby towns) to find out what is going on in your area. Reading the Friday or Saturday Life section of a newspaper also will give you information about local events. I have also known couples who have thumbed through the yellow pages to get ideas for things they could do on a date. I have known couples who stopped by hotels to go through the brochures for area sites or events. They sorted out the ones they liked and made going-out plans to these events or locations.

If these ideas expand your going-out repertoire,

great! Write down a few ideas for going out. Each spouse should make his or her own list.

Well, now you have it all. You know what a going-out lifestyle is and how it helps a relationship: we spend much of the week working and serving each other, our children, friends, and church. But going out helps us do all of this with a much better attitude and reduces the risk of burnout.

The Ten-Minute Marriage Principle keeps couples heart to heart. Going out keeps them hand in hand as well.

13

SHOW ME THE MONEY

Money is a hot topic for most couples. It's said that couples fight mostly about money and sex. I think money is such a big issue because it's a symbol and measure of how we think or feel. If you open someone's checkbook or credit card statement, you can get a great idea of the person's priorities and values.

When a friend of mine lost his grandmother, the family went through her papers. Her checkbook looked like a who's who of television ministries. She wasn't a wealthy woman, but month after month she gave a certain amount to each ministry. You could easily see her heart to give and help others through her spending.

You see, how we spend our money reflects, to a degree, our hearts, as Jesus pointed out: "Where your treasure is, there your heart will be also" (Matt. 6:21). Finances are definitely a muscle in your marriage that you want to be fit. You don't want to be a couple who love God but don't pay their bills! You and your spouse can become a competent financial team. If you do so, you'll create harmony, which will enhance your use of the Ten-Minute Marriage Principle and the accompanying intimacy exercises.

I'm sure you've already discovered that marriage and money make for interesting dynamics. You know the way God seems to put together one person who likes the bedroom window open and one who likes it closed? Well, my experience is that usually God places two different financial personalities together too.

Take Cameron and Liz. Cameron came from a financially prudent family. He was taught to tithe, save, and invest and that money had a purpose. So Cameron worked hard, saved 30 percent of his check, and tithed. He decided he didn't need to live on all his money since his expenses were low—for example, his used car was paid for.

Liz grew up in a family where money was a real mystery. Dad seemed to make more than enough. Mom bought whatever she wanted and their princess, Liz, never lacked for anything, even during college.

Liz and Cameron met and fell in love their last year of college. Their dating and wedding went smoothly, but as you can imagine, after the honeymoon they faced day-to-day financial issues that constantly drained them. Both felt exhausted by their arguments and neither felt understood. (I know you probably can't relate to this.)

Couples have to navigate financial waters *together*. Just like spirituality, sexuality, social circles, and parenting, finances are a real adventure. To successfully manage money, couples need to be in agreement on the major issues. It's perfectly normal to disagree. After all, you're both intelligent adults with strong opinions and different backgrounds. But your marriage won't be happy if you don't settle these issues as soon as possible.

So let's jump in so that you can maximize your Ten-Minute Marriage Principle lifestyle. If you tackle the larger money issues and can move toward agreement, you will have fewer arguments and, in many cases, more money over a lifetime.

TITHING

I am not going to give a lengthy explanation or position on tithing; I have learned that's futile. Money is often more emotional than intellectual for many people. Rather I want to share a few things with you that may help.

Lisa and I have tithed our entire marriage. Actually we do more than tithe. I was saved by Christ so radically from a lifestyle of shameful behavior that I feel strongly about showing love back to Him. I am a lover by nature and to love is to give: "For God so loved the world that he gave his one and only Son" (John 3:16). God loves, and so God gives. It is actually that simple for me.

I believe Jesus tithed in His life partly because He liked to give. Jesus also tithed because it was required by the Law—had He not tithed, He would have sinned. Of course He also offered Himself as an offering. So tithing is an easy lifestyle to choose for the One who chose to give His whole life away.

Giving 10 percent (more or less) to a local church is a great idea. Giving more to organizations or ministries you want to fuel is also a great idea. Let me tell you something as a counselor who has talked to many, many couples: every couple I have met who had significant money issues did not tithe. I also know many million-aires across the country, and I've found that they usually not only tithe, they make giving a lifestyle.

Couples have to agree on this issue, so they have to discuss it, sometimes at length. It's important that they agree since they share in the results of this decision. Here you might consider utilizing some of the earlier support principles we have discussed. Do you remember which government you are? Do you have some financial teammates you can call for advice? Since tithing is a lifestyle choice for your family, don't be concerned if you need several conversations to find agreement about the details.

Take out a new piece of paper and fill out these sentences:

The date we discussed tithing was _____.

As a couple we agreed to ____ tithe ____ not to tithe.

The Practical Side

There are very practical issues that each couple needs to address so that money does not become a source of contention in the relationship. I will address some of the basic questions, and as I move from one topic to another, feel free to stop and discuss any issues you have on this topic.

I realize that for some of you this section will be a walk in the park. You have already had most of these discussions and have figured these issues out for yourselves. Some of you, however, are right in the middle of these problems. So let's grapple with each question and option to facilitate this conversation going as smoothly as possible.

WHOSE MONEY IS IT?

That's right—this first question must be settled so as to make the rest of the money conversation make sense. I have met countless couples who never were clear on this question during their marriages. If one spouse works, does that spouse own the money, or is it joint money and the couple should make joint decisions?

Actually the money is God's, on loan to the couple to manage well. Have you ever thought of it this way? Discuss who actually owns the money.

- ☐ God
- ☐ He does
- ☐ She does
- ☐ We both do

WHO MAKES THE FINANCIAL DECISIONS?

I realize that for time purposes, or because one spouse is more "gifted" in this area than the other, a husband *or* wife may actually sit down and write the monthly checks. Some couples actually write all the checks together, but in my experience that isn't usually the case.

The problem with having one person write the checks is that he or she can get the idea he or she is Lord of the Money. To minimize this happening, I want to ask you as a couple to think about what amount of money will require both spouses' input before it's spent? Let me give you some ideas.

- ☐ On large decisions only
- ☐ On investments
- ☐ On purchases over $_____
- ☐ On most financial decisions

WHAT ROLE DOES THE "NONFINANCIAL" SPOUSE PLAY?

Is the person who doesn't write the checks expected to have any real knowledge of the business side of the marriage? Here are some options to discuss expectations regarding the "nonfinancial" spouse:

- ☐ He or she is blissfully ignorant (has no responsibility).
  Can spend as he/she wishes?
  Has a cap on spending?
- ☐ He or she must connect occasionally with the "bookkeeper" so as to be aware of the couple's financial condition.
  Will it be a weekly meeting?
  Will it be a bimonthly meeting?
  Will it be a monthly meeting?
  Will it be a quarterly meeting?
- ☐ He or she will be included in the financial issues on a need-to-know basis only.

HOW WILL WE WILL KEEP TRACK OF WHERE THE MONEY GOES?

Some people really like keeping track of numbers. Some do it out of a need to be responsible, and some avoid this like the plague.

Regardless of the natural gifts you have as a couple, you need to address this issue of tracking finances together. Here are some options for keeping track:

☐   Use a checkbook and credit card statements.
☐   Use a computer program like QuickBooks.
☐   Other _____

WILL WE HAVE A BUDGET?

"To budget or not to budget: that is the question." That's my spin on the famous question asked by Shakespeare's Hamlet. Sometimes couples settle on a budget and live by it strictly, and sometimes it's an idea couples just talk about. Let's just settle this one to see what you really want to do.

☐   We will have absolutely no budget.
☐   We will maintain a loose budget.
☐   We will use a structured budget but will not keep track of each other's decisions.
☐   We will abide by a structured budget, and we're accountable to each other for the financial decisions we make.

HOW MUCH OF OUR INCOME SHOULD WE LIVE ON?

Now here is a really big question. When I ask an American Christian couple how much money they should live on, they look at me as if I am from Mars. After a moment of silence, I'll get answers like 110 percent, 100 percent, or some might say 90 percent.

Hang with me here for a moment. This feeling of needing to spend every dime we make is real. This discussion usually starts the first month of marriage. Perhaps you both made so little money prior to marriage, the question never even entered your young minds—so you think, *Of course we need to spend every dime in order to make it.*

If we are not careful, however, this attitude toward spending can put us on a slippery slope of earning, spending, creating debt, and arguments. Think for a minute about the big financial issues that face most couples:

Saving for the first house

Car purchase and maintenance

Housing

Family health care

Vacations

Christmas

College

Retirement

Parent care

With the bigger picture in mind, you can easily see you will need a whole pile of money in the future. Most couples make more money as they age. If, however, you spend everything you earn, you won't have any money when you need it.

Talk about what percent of your income, or actual number of dollars, should go toward some of these major areas on a monthly basis. Write these out on a piece of paper:

Tithe   _____ percent or $_____

Auto   _____ percent or $_____

Housing   _____ percent or $_____

Family health care   _____ percent or $_____

Vacation   _____ percent or $_____

Christmas   _____ percent or $_____

College   _____ percent or $_____

Retirement   _____ percent or $_____

Parental Care   _____ percent or $_____

Don't get depressed! I know that if you have been on the earn-and-spend plan, the idea of deliberately curbing spending can be really painful. But in the long run, it's wise, and you'll be really glad you did it.

These issues may challenge you, but that's all right. If you need help, seek out your financial teammate(s). You might need some mentoring in this area to make financial planning a lifestyle.

The earlier you smooth out the possible financial bumps, the better for you both. Imagine living within your means, creating more wealth monthly, and feeling more secure about your future. You can experience this if you settle your financial lifestyle now.

INCOME VS. WEALTH

Here is a fun aspect of financial planning. This one will provoke some thought. I want to have a brief conversation about income and wealth. Income is a relatively basic concept. You hire yourself out by the hour or salary to someone, and that person or company gives you a certain amount of money at the agreed-upon frequency. You are expected to work hard and be loyal. More money will (usually) result.

Most Americans live in the income reality. Wealth, however, is a totally different lifestyle. Wealth creates money without one's working a nine-to-five job, though some work is usually involved.

Those with a wealth mind-set search for ways to create wealth, such as buying or starting companies, real estate, and investing. There are endless ways to create wealth in America. If you are just making it day by day, the idea of creating wealth can be difficult. If, however, you start saving or investing money, you will have capital to put a down payment on a business, real estate, or other venture. As that venture pays for itself, you can move to the next one and so on.

This is a marriage book and not a wealth book. But how a couple thinks about income and wealth can make a huge difference in their lives. This alone will impact how they live month to month and what they're looking forward to in the future. Ideally, you start with income and then start creating wealth on the side. Over time, the wealth equals the income and then you can decide if you want to work at your job too. Even if you stay employed, you will feel freer because you know you don't have to be there.

Discuss these concepts together. Discuss where you are now, where you want to be in the future, and how you might experiment to get to your agreed-upon goal.

Take a moment and check off where you currently are on the income versus wealth continuum.

☐ Right now, we live on income only.
☐ Right now, we live on income and are building wealth on the side.
☐ Right now, we have no income but exist on the wealth we created.

You may be perfectly comfortable where you are. You as a couple might also want to make some adjustments since you are thinking about this now. Check the box you want to work toward.

☐ We want to live on income only.

☐ We want to live on income and create wealth.

☐ We want to live only on the wealth we create.

If you want to move from income only toward income and wealth, you need to build some savings. How much can you start saving so you have some money to make money with?

We can save $_____ a month to begin moving from an income-only lifestyle to a income-and-wealth lifestyle.

If you are moving from income only to income and wealth, what strategies do you want to investigate at this time?

☐ Business

☐ Real Estate

☐ Investing

☐ Other _____

I hope you had some fun just thinking outside your current box. I find it a very helpful exercise to get couples to evaluate where they are and where they want to be financially. I know you will find this support principle of income and wealth to be very helpful in your marriage. Fill out these sentences on your piece of paper:

We had our discussion on income and wealth on _____

_____. We decided to _____

_____.

MARRIAGE INVESTMENT

The next topic you should discuss is the amount of money you want to spend on your marriage. Many couples do not sit down and plan what they will spend to enhance their relationships. There are several good ways to invest in your marriage. What's exciting is that today it is acceptable and even applauded if couples spend to sustain great marriages!

First, discuss going out. You can read the chapter on going out and decide the value of that lifestyle to you as a couple. How much money, on a monthly basis, will you invest in going out? I use investing intentionally. Many of Lisa's and my favorite memories since having children are our nights of going out together.

Overnight outings can also enhance your marriage. You know: just the two of you go to a hotel or bed-and-breakfast and spend time being lovers and friends. "Overnights" also require discussion if you want to put money aside for them.

Books, DVDs, and other marriage enrichment materials are also a great idea. It's very helpful for a couple to be stimulated with new ideas, approaches, and humor about marriage. Even as an author of three marriage books, I like to receive insights other couples have gleaned and tools to better love and appreciate the daughter of God, my Lisa. These materials cost money. You can decide if this is part of your marriage investing as well.

Marriage conferences can be very stimulating to your relationship and are another financial consideration. You can discuss these and decide if annually you will participate in a marriage conference or two. If conferences aren't held locally, this may involve some travel as well. If you can't travel, one option is marriage conference DVDs.

Over the course of your marriage, you will manage hundreds of thousands of dollars. Deciding to invest in the relationship of a lifetime is a great idea.

If you are able to complete discussions in all these areas and agree on plans and priorities, congratulations! You did it! You rode the rapids of marriage and money. Hopefully you see some things more clearly or from a different perspective. I also hope your money decisions make you more of a team in marriage.

In addition to the Ten-Minute Marriage Principle, I want to give you ideas and tools to be successful financially both short- and long-term. Money is meant to be a blessing, and marriage is meant to be a blessing. To have both a good marriage and a sound financial plan is a double blessing. Enjoy both of your blessings today and for the many years ahead of you.

14

DINNER'S READY

Our minds can conjure up pictures of our mothers calling down the hall or up the steps one of our favorite sayings: "Dinner's ready!" We all are glad that when Mom and Dad decided to have us, they also made a covenant to feed us. I'm sure they had no idea at the time just how much work would be involved in providing our three squares a day.

When you have children, you make all kinds of covenants that involve perhaps unexpected amounts of work. As married people, we also make many covenants to our spouses. These covenants range from relating to our in-laws to money, housing, children, and let's not forget, sex. That's right; sex is one of these covenants that we make when we get married.

When we were walking down the aisle, most of us were probably thinking about sex. Of course, we were blessed to see our spouses all dressed up and say those great vows to us. We liked the get-together afterwards, the food, the friends, the laughter, but still there was the hopeful thought of sex.

Praise God for sex! So many couples have issues related to sex that I thought it was important that we spend some time on this subject. Your sex life can soar to great new heights as you implement the Ten-Minute Marriage Principle. The exercises will cause you to grow closer, and that new intimacy can lead to greater frequency as well as great satisfaction in sex. I want you to have a great sex life and so does God. After all, the first command of God to mammals was to go forth and multiply, which means to have sex.

Remember, it's God, not the devil, who made sex. Sex was in the heart of God before God even made Eve. Adam was made sexual in the image of God long before Eve was on the scene. Eve was made sexual in the image of God before she was brought to the man. When you think of it, almost every godly person in the Bible had sex. You can just read the first chapter of Matthew if you don't believe me. Remember that when someone "begat" someone, he or she had to have sex.

I want you to know God's heart on the matter of sex. He's okay with it and it's best if we are okay with sex as well. After all, as with cooking, we will spend thousands of hours on it (praise God!).

Before we go any further, let me make perfectly clear that I don't want you to have a ten-minute sex life! Rather I want you to have a great sexual connection spiritually, emotionally, and physically.

THE DESIGN

Remember all those exercises we talked about earlier in the book? When you spend that ten minutes connecting outside the bedroom, you are preparing yourself for a greater sex life. Many couples are surprised at how much better their sex lives are because of what they are doing *outside* the bedroom.

I am currently not much of a sports spectator. Don't get me wrong, I like sports, but I'd rather run, work out, ride a bike, or shoot some basketball myself than watch other people sweat. In junior high when I played football, it was great. We did all these exercises, calisthenics, running, hitting, and scrimmaging. We put in many hours of practice to play well.

Your Ten-Minute Exercises are just like those warm-up exercises. They are fun all by themselves, but the results in the bedroom make all those ten-minute dailies worth it.

Let's walk through the basics of the who, what, where, how often, and when of sex. It's wise to sit down and intelligently make some basic decisions. Sex is a subject that many couples have difficulty discussing without injury.

I want you to be able to connect sexually and manage it in a way that brings peace to the relationship. You see, when a couple doesn't really sit down and talk through these issues, they tend toward manipulation and chaos. Both spouses learn tactics of engaging or avoiding that are pretty primitive.

For example, she rushes to bed before he does and falls asleep. He can't wake her up and ask her for sex, so her manipulation to get out of sex was successful. Then there is the guy's manipulation: he asks all the time to increase his odds. He manipulates his chances by believing that asking for more leads to more sex.

So since we are competent adults, we can also be competent sexually. As we talk through this subject, stay openhearted, because some of these ideas can set you free from primitive traditions you may have created in your marriage. For this discussion, I am going to use dinner as my analogy. Why? Because we can all relate to food, and I think it makes people more comfortable with this topic.

WHAT'S FOR DINNER?

After all, what's for dinner is a very important discussion to have. I know some of us want an expert to say this or that is totally off-limits. A man will ask relationship or sex experts about a particular sexual behavior. He wants to hear that his idea is a good one. Then he can report it to his wife and shame her for not doing it.

Unbeknownst to this man, his wife also consults relationship or sex experts on the same question. She's hoping the experts will say that such and such behavior is not acceptable. She is just as sincere as her husband. She also will report her findings to her husband to support why she doesn't have to participate in this certain behavior and shame him for suggesting such a thing.

Let me show you a better way of negotiating what's for dinner. We are going to eat (you know what I mean, have sex). So let's talk about actually all the elements of the sex life: who, what, where, how often, and when.

WHO

First off, there are absolutely *no guests* at this "meal." That means no third persons or any pornography is acceptable as part of your sex life. These can hurt a marriage incredibly. I can't tell you how many Christians have tried these behaviors and damaged their relationships for years. The "who" of your soup should include only you and your spouse, period.

WHAT

Some people love Italian food, others like prime rib, still others like seafood, Asian dishes, or Mexican food. It's true there may be people who eat only one type of food their entire lives. From a nutritional standpoint, eating only one food isn't very healthy. It's also not very creative.

Remember that we serve a creative God. He could have made only one plant, say seaweed, which would have been the only food all humans could harvest and digest. Thank God He didn't make just one food or just one sexual flavor, but that we get to enjoy variety instead!

So what kind of "food" do you want to "eat"? What you want and what you can mutually agree upon may be different, but let's go ahead and decide what you'd like in your soup, so to speak. Maybe you want carrots, maybe some chicken or steak, maybe potatoes, or maybe not.

1. *Make a list.* Grab two pens and two tablets. Each spouse should write down the ingredients he or she would like to have in his or her soup. That's right: make a list of the positions or behaviors that are acceptable for your "soup." Be careful not to list ingredients you already know are not going to be part of your soup. Also, list only positions or behaviors you can physically perform without injury! As we age, our minds may be more flexible and stronger than our bodies.

2. *Combine your lists.* You may have a couple of ideas that you need to discuss to see if they'll make it into the soup. On these ingredients, be clear what you are talking about—describe the act or position in detail. Otherwise you can't decide intelligently on whether to do it.

3. *Vote on ingredients.* You have three types of votes when voting on an ingredient. You can vote Yes, meaning you think that ingredient is a great addition to the soup. You can vote Sometimes, which means you might not want to have this ingredient regularly, but you don't mind serving your spouse in this way sometimes. And you can vote No.

If one spouse votes Sometimes and the other person votes Yes, they will need to define "Sometimes." Does this ingredient happen weekly, monthly, quarterly, annually, or on every tenth anniversary? If you are not clear here, you might have some misunderstandings later on.

If one spouse votes No and the other Yes, enjoy what you both agree upon and discuss this option at a future time.

Now, who brings the ingredient to the bedroom?

Knowing who is responsible to initiate this ingredient is also important to determine. If the wife or husband agrees to be the initiator of this particular act or position, he or she should keep his or her word on bringing this ingredient cheerfully.

After you finish this process, you will know what's for dinner. Next you'll want to know where dinner is.

WHERE

Most of us have our "meals" in the bedroom. But those years before children, after children, and when they are not around can allow for some creativity in where you have sex. People's sense of adventure flows over into their sex lives. If you are married to a creative spouse, this is not a curse but a blessing. You should find a middle ground that stretches you both. If you are married to a person who prefers safety over adventure, this is also a blessing. I don't know why these two married, but it happens regularly. I think it's God's way of allowing us the opportunity to be patient with each other and to grow.

1. Make a list. Take out two separate pieces of paper and each of you write out options for where to "eat dinner" besides the bedroom.

One spouse may like to have a sexual meal by the fireplace or in the shower or bathtub. Some couples have outside adventures or hotel adventures. Do not, however, risk exposing yourself to others in the process. Be creative and flexible, and yet honor both people in the relationship.

Remember that God is a creative God, and if you need creativity, ask God! Yes, it's okay to ask God for ideas and fun. Don't underestimate how creativity can enhance your relationship. Remember the creative God we serve!

2. Combine your lists. Put all of your ideas together.

3. Vote on options. After you have listed possible places you would like, it's time to vote. If one of you has a few more creative ideas, vote on these. Again, you can vote Yes, No, or Sometimes. If you get stuck, you can vote to try an idea once, flip a coin, or just accept you are not in agreement and let the matter rest.

HOW OFTEN

Yes, we do have to talk about how often you both would like to have sex. Rarely do I meet a couple where the man and woman want exactly the same frequency. Before discussing this with your spouse, consider a few things:

Your ages and any medical conditions

Your work schedules

Your children's needs

Your social obligations

What your spouse needs to be ready for sex

If you need to adjust to a frequency that meets both partners' needs, start the negotiating process with your spouse. *Negotiate* means that it's not polite to make it all about you. If one person wants dinner once a week and the other person wants it three times, then go to two or rotate: have sex once a week one week, then have it three times the next week. This may be tricky and sensitive; if you can't resolve this on your own, you might want to seek counseling to successfully resolve the sexual frequency issue in your marriage.

WHEN

Now that you have negotiated how often you are going to have dinner, let's move to when. Every couple resolves this differently. Some pick certain days of the week, others split the week into segments. One person gets this part of the week, and the other gets the other part of the week. Others give each other so many days to initiate sex, then the next day becomes the other person's turn. Regardless of how you decide this, it is important to agree.

It is really important that both people initiate sex. Ladies should ask their husbands for sex as often as men ask their wives. Don't revert to "It's not my personality to do that." God made both spouses sexual in His image. So be godly and initiate love and sex. This is critical to having a healthy sex life.

Write down your decisions in all of these areas. Couples who can agree on who is involved in the soup making, what is in their sexual soup, where they enjoy soup, how often they have soup, when soup will be on the menu, will do much better in marriage than those who guess or never plan. You will have sex thousands of times over the decades, and this is supposed to be a blessing.

If the sexual area can be worked out in a marriage, you can both be more fulfilled, more relaxed, and have a whole lot less sexual anxiety interfering with your intimacy.

New Dishes

Most of us have our favorite restaurants. In these restaurants, we even have our favorite dishes. For example, every time I go to the Cheesecake Factory I order the same dish, the Bang-Bang Chicken and Shrimp. It's great! Although ordering the same meal is an okay way to do life, sometimes it's also healthy to try new dishes on a menu.

It's good for us once in a while to try a new dish, just to see if we would like it as much or even better. I can't tell you how many times I've gone to a restaurant and my favorite dish was unavailable or it was no longer on the menu, so I had to choose something else. On many of these occasions, I have been pleasantly surprised. Sometimes I realized I didn't like the new dish and wouldn't order it again, but at least I tried it.

You know where I am going with this conversation. It is occasionally good for you to try a new "dish" sexually. You can settle into your standard meal and that's great, but once in a while, mix it up a little bit. You might even plan to try something new monthly, quarterly, or annually. You have already established what is and isn't in your sexual soup so you know what the limitations are, but again, you can be creative about your sex life.

I realize that one or both of you might have some trepidation here. You may have control, fear, or other issues that make you anxious about experimenting. God can help you stretch, and you can always try something new with the option to change your mind later. That being said, there are some things that may just not have any appeal to you or may feel somewhat violating. If you feel an act, location, or position is violating, then I strongly suggest you talk to a counselor before experimenting with it. If it's just different, then you might want to give it a try.

Using creativity can stimulate sexual growth over a lifetime. I know some people want exactly the same item every time. Rarely, however, do both people want the same meal even if it is a wonderful meal. Staying creative allows both people to grow sexually for a lifetime.

For some, sexual issues are a breeze, and for others, they're very difficult. As you've done the Ten-Minute Marriage Principle Exercises, though, you've probably seen some results in the intimacy of your relationship by now. If discipline gives results, try using it with some of the support principles here in our discussion on sex.

KIDS TO BED

I want to share with you a little theory I have. I think God designed men to put their kids to bed. Now hear me out. I am not saying moms should never put children to bed. But when a mother puts her children to bed, it's often an event or experience. The mother usually comes out of these little people's bedrooms more tired than she was when she went in.

When a man puts children to bed, it's a totally different dynamic. He reads the same Bible story, prays with them, and even talks a little about their day. Yet he will not come out any more tired than when he went in (especially if he knows sex is going to happen).

There is something else that's different. When a man tells his child to stay in bed, there is a certain clarity for the child. I think subliminally the child hears from the father something like, "Stay in bed or it may be the end of your life." I'm not sure how it works, but children usually stay in bed, and Dad is able to change gears and be a lover to his wife.

I realize this could occur in reverse in your family: Dad is the softy and Mom holds the line. I can only share with you what my experience has been, and that is when Dad says "Good night," activity ceases. There is a finality to those words that Hadassah and Jubal, and yes, even Moses, have come to understand.

Women take longer to switch gears from caretaker of children to lover of a man. So, husband, here's some free advice: tell your wife you'll take the children tonight. Suggest she go relax, take a bath, read a magazine, or whatever she needs to do to help her prepare for you.

Then you will go to bed with a relaxed, prepared woman who probably likes you a little more because you showed you cared for her well-being and the children's well-being too. Caring goes a long way with women.

It's just a theory, guys, but try it for a month. See if there are any changes when your wife can rely on you to do the last lap of the day with the children. It's a great time for you to check in with your children as well. So in this theory everybody wins. You feel like a better husband and father, she feels you are caring, and the kids get to deepen their relationships with you.

THE SEX ENEMY

When I'm teaching a men's conference, I ask if any are addicted to pornography or sex. Half the men will raise their hands. Many have tried to get better but failed, so they spend many years living a double life filled with shame. I know women can also have a pornography or fantasy sex issue as well, yet I see it most prevalent among men.

Why is sexual and pornographic addiction such an epidemic? First, our culture has had a sexual revolution in which pornography has become mainstream. Many men today have been educated sexually by pornography. I also believe this epidemic is happening because nobody is asking two difficult questions. Men are not asking men these questions and wives are not asking their husbands these questions.

You can ask your husband (or if you are a man, you can ask friends) right now:

When was the last time you saw pornography?

When was the last time you masturbated?

Wife, be prepared. Do not assume that your husband is perfectly okay about avoiding these behaviors. If you ask your husband these questions, you might get answers that shock you. You have a 50 percent chance of getting an answer that may present recent activity in either or both areas.

If you do get an unwanted answer and discover the enemy has been trapping your husband, remember that you are not to blame. It's not your body, sex life, or relationship that made him masturbate or look at porn. In most cases this trap began back when he was a teenager. On our Web site *www.intimatematters.com,* you can find helpful resources for you or your husband.

There are only a few men, twenty-three to be exact, out of the tens of thousands I have spoken to who haven't masturbated or seen pornography at some point in their lives. Sadly, most men set themselves up to fail. Instead of waiting for marriage, they get attached to porn and fantasy as young men and suffer silently.

The Internet has made this problem much worse. Every home should have a porn blocker. When you go online, you are connecting to the world's largest, most perverse porn store. If you don't have a porn blocker, go to *www.tenminutemarriage.com* and download a free trial today. Your family needs to be safe from this enemy.

If you have asked your husband these questions and found out that he has trouble in these areas, we have free newsletters and many more resources to help your marriage get rid of public enemy number one. As a couple, you can look over the section on addictions in chapter 9 to discover if your husband's problem has reached this level. If you need support group information for your area, we keep a national directory of Christian sexual recovery groups. Be encouraged. There is much help for both the addicted spouse and his wife.

IN SUMMARY

Let me remind you: don't make dinner—build a sex life—without doing the Ten-Minute Exercises. If a man tries to get his wife to set up sexual agreements without doing the daily marriage exercises, his wife will rightfully feel defrauded. I tell wives not to agree on sexual management until at least they have completed thirty days of doing the Ten-Minute Exercises.

Once you've started a new habit of deeper communication, then you can negotiate, play, and try new things for "dinner." Be encouraged that when you can lovingly negotiate these matters, your relationship will have less stress and more peace. *Bon appétit!*

You have covered so much ground in these pages! If you do your core exercises and back them up with the support principles I've offered, you will be amazed at what your relationship becomes. You can now identify relationship problems and move toward solutions and goals. Your marriage will become both joyous and resilient, full of momentum to last a lifetime.

You've earned the absolute best marriage possible. Work hard, have fun, and spread the strength of your marriage to all you love!

FEELINGS EXERCISE

1. I feel _____ (put word here) when _____ (put a present situation when you feel this).

2. I first remember feeling _____ (put the same feeling word here) when _____ (explain earliest occurrence of this feeling).

Abandoned	Alienated	Appreciated	Awestruck
Abused	Alive	Appreciative	Badgered
Accepted	Alluring	Apprehensive	Baited
Accepting	Alone	Appropriate	Bashful
Accused	Aloof	Approved	Battered
Aching	Amazed	Argumentative	Beaten
Admired	Amused	Aroused	Beautiful
Adored	Angry	Assertive	Belittled
Adventurous	Anguished	Astonished	Belligerent
Affectionate	Annoyed	Attached	Bereaved
Aggravated	Anxious	Attacked	Betrayed
Aggressive	Apart	Attentive	Bewildered
Agony	Apathetic	Attractive	Blamed
Agreeable	Apologetic	Aware	Blaming

Bonded	Courageous	Distressed	Funny
Bored	Courteous	Distrusted	Furious
Bothered	Coy	Distrustful	Generous
Brave	Crabby	Disturbed	Gentle
Breathless	Cranky	Dominated	Genuine
Bristling	Crazy	Domineering	Giddy
Broken-up	Creative	Doomed	Giving
Bruised	Critical	Doubtful	Goofy
Bubbly	Criticized	Dreadful	Grateful
Burdened	Cross	Eager	Greedy
Burned	Crushed	Ecstatic	Grief
Callous	Cuddly	Edified	Grim
Calm	Curious	Edgy	Grimy
Capable	Cut	Elated	Grouchy
Captivated	Damned	Embarrassed	Grumpy
Carefree	Dangerous	Empowered	Hard
Careful	Daring	Empty	Harried
Careless	Dead	Enraged	Hassled
Caring	Deceived	Enraptured	Healthy
Cautious	Deceptive	Enthusiastic	Helpful
Certain	Defensive	Enticed	Helpless
Chased	Delicate	Esteemed	Hesitant
Cheated	Delighted	Exasperated	High
Cheerful	Demeaned	Excited	Hollow
Childlike	Demoralized	Exhilarated	Honest
Choked-up	Dependent	Exposed	Hopeful
Close	Depressed	Fake	Hopeless
Cold	Deprived	Fascinated	Horrified
Comfortable	Deserted	Feisty	Hostile
Comforted	Desirable	Ferocious	Humiliated
Competent	Desired	Foolish	Hurried
Competitive	Despair	Forced	Hurt
Complacent	Despondent	Forceful	Hyper
Complete	Destroyed	Forgiven	Ignorant
Confident	Different	Forgotten	Ignored
Confused	Dirty	Free	Immature
Considerate	Disenchanted	Friendly	Impatient
Consumed	Disgusted	Frightened	Important
Content	Disinterested	Frustrated	Impotent
Cool	Dispirited	Full	Impressed

Incompetent	Mystified	Raped	Selfish
Incomplete	Nasty	Ravished	Sensuous
Independent	Nervous	Ravishing	Separated
Innocent	Nice	Real	Sexy
Insecure	Numb	Refreshed	Shattered
Insignificant	Nurtured	Regretful	Shocked
Insincere	Nuts	Rejected	Shot down
Inspired	Obsessed	Rejecting	Shy
Insulted	Offended	Rejuvenated	Sickened
Interested	Open	Relaxed	Silly
Intimate	Ornery	Relieved	Sincere
Intolerant	Out of Control	Remarkable	Sinking
Involved	Overcome	Remembered	Smart
Irate	Overjoyed	Removed	Smothered
Irked	Overpowered	Repressed	Smug
Irrational	Overwhelmed	Repulsed	Sneaky
Irresponsible	Pampered	Repulsive	Snowed
Irritable	Panicked	Resentful	Soft
Irritated	Paralyzed	Resistant	Solid
Isolated	Paranoid	Respected	Solitary
Jealous	Patient	Responsible	Sorry
Jittery	Peaceful	Responsive	Spacey
Joyous	Pensive	Restless	Special
Lively	Perceptive	Revolved	Spiteful
Lonely	Perturbed	Riled	Spontaneous
Loose	Phony	Rotten	Squelched
Lost	Pleasant	Ruined	Starved
Loving	Pleased	Sad	Stiff
Low	Positive	Safe	Stifled
Lucky	Powerless	Satiated	Stimulated
Lustful	Precious	Satisfied	Strangled
Mad	Present	Scared	Strong
Malicious	Pressured	Scolded	Stubborn
Maudlin	Pretty	Scorned	Stuck
Mean	Proud	Scrutinized	Stunned
Miserable	Pulled apart	Secure	Stupid
Misunderstood	Put down	Seduced	Subdued
Moody	Puzzled	Seductive	Submissive
Morose	Quarrelsome	Self-centered	Successful
Mournful	Quiet	Self-conscious	Suffocated

Sure	Tortured	Unfriendly	Violent
Sweet	Touched	Ungrateful	Vulnerable
Sympathy	Trapped	Unhappy	Warm
Tainted	Tremendous	Unified	Wary
Tearful	Tricked	Unimpressed	Weak
Tender	Trusted	Unsafe	Whipped
Tense	Trustful	Unstable	Whole
Terrific	Trusting	Unworthy	Wicked
Terrified	Ugly	Upset	Wild
Thrilled	Unacceptable	Uptight	Willing
Ticked	Unapproachable	Used	Wiped out
Tickled	Unaware	Useful	Wishful
Tight	Uncertain	Useless	Withdrawn
Timid	Uncomfortable	Validated	Wonderful
Tired	Under control	Valuable	Worried
Tolerant	Understanding	Valued	Worthy
Tormented	Understood	Victorious	
Torn	Undesirable	Violated	

From Douglas Weiss, *Intimacy: A 100-Day Guide to Lasting Relationships* (Lake Mary, FL: Siloam Press, 2001, 2003), 341–343. Used by permission.

APPENDIX B

EXAMPLES OF *WINNING@MARRIAGE* GAME QUESTIONS

- What is your spouse's pet name for you?
- What is your spouse's favorite Scripture?
- What characteristic do you admire most in your spouse?
- At what age did your spouse become a Christian?
- Who is most likely to make your spouse feel inspired?
- What is the latest compliment you received from your spouse?
- What was your first vacation after your honeymoon?
- What is your spouse's favorite article of clothing?
- What is your spouse's favorite hiding place for presents?

- What is the oldest piece of furniture in your home?
- What is your spouse's favorite section of the paper to read?
- What is your spouse's biggest pet peeve?
- What flavor was your wedding cake?
- What one item does your spouse have that he or she has kept since childhood?
- What is a tradition that is unique to your family?

APPENDIX C

CHARTS FOR TEN-MINUTE EXERCISES

DAY	1.	2.	3.
1.			
2.			
3.			
4.			
5.			
6.			
7.			
8.			
9.			
10.			
11.			
12.			

DAY	1.	2.	3.
13.			
14.			
15.			
16.			
17.			
18.			
19.			
20.			
21.			
22.			
23.			
24.			
25.			
26.			
27.			
28.			
29.			
30.			

DAY	1.	2.	3.
1.			
2.			
3.			
4.			
5.			
6.			
7.			
8.			
9.			
10.			
11.			
12.			
13.			
14.			
15.			
16.			
17.			
18.			
19.			
20.			
21.			
22.			

DAY	1.	2.	3.
23.			
24.			
25.			
26.			
27.			
28.			
29.			
30.			

DAY	1.	2.	3.
1.			
2.			
3.			
4.			
5.			
6.			
7.			
8.			
9.			
10.			
11.			
12.			
13.			

DAY	1.	2.	3.
14.			
15.			
16.			
17.			
18.			
19.			
20.			
21.			
22.			
23.			
24.			
25.			
26.			
27.			
28.			
29.			
30.			

ABOUT THE AUTHOR

Dr. Douglas Weiss has published sixteen books on sexuality and marriage and has also produced numerous CD and DVD products that have sold over one hundred thousand copies combined. Dr. Weiss currently serves as the executive director for Heart to Heart Counseling Center in Colorado Springs and speaks at many national and international conferences each year. He and his wife, Lisa, have been married for twenty years. You can visit his Web site at *www.tenminutemarriage.com* or contact Heart to Heart Counseling Center at 719-278-3708.